S0-CQS-880

Supervised study & Literature

INGLIS LECTURES
IN SECONDARY EDUCATION

TRENDS IN AMERICAN SECONDARY ED-
UCATION. By Leonard V. Koos. 1925.
$1.00

OPPORTUNITY AND ACCOMPLISHMENT IN
SECONDARY EDUCATION. By Paul H.
Hanus. 1926. $1.00

DO AMERICANS REALLY VALUE EDUCA-
TION? By Abraham Flexner. 1927.
$1.00

THE UNIQUE CHARACTER OF AMERICAN
SECONDARY EDUCATION. By Charles
H. Judd. 1928. $1.00

SECONDARY EDUCATION AND INDUSTRI-
ALISM. By George S. Counts. 1929.
$1.00

THE GREAT INVESTMENT. By Thomas
H. Briggs. 1930. $1.50

THE GREAT INVESTMENT

SECONDARY EDUCATION IN A DEMOCRACY

LONDON : HUMPHREY MILFORD

OXFORD UNIVERSITY PRESS

The Inglis Lecture, 1930

THE GREAT INVESTMENT

SECONDARY EDUCATION IN A DEMOCRACY

Because one truth leads right to the world's end. — BROWNING

BY

THOMAS H. BRIGGS

Teachers College, Columbia University

LA
222
B78
1931

CAMBRIDGE

HARVARD UNIVERSITY PRESS

1930

28159

COPYRIGHT, 1930

BY THE PRESIDENT AND FELLOWS OF

HARVARD COLLEGE

First edition March 6, 1930
Second edition, April 1, 1930
Third edition, August 11, 1931

PRINTED AT THE NORWOOD PRESS,

NORWOOD, MASS., U.S.A.

ALEXANDRO INGLIS
VIRO CONSTANTISSIMO DOCTISSIMO
MAGISTRO
TAM AD COGITANDUM SEVERO
QUAM AD SUADENDUM DOCENDUMVE
STRENUO
DULCI DECORI AMICORUM
AMICO ET IPSI DULCISSIMO

THE
INGLIS LECTURESHIP

To honor the memory of Alexander Inglis, 1879–1924, his friends and colleagues gave to the Graduate School of Education, Harvard University, a fund for the maintenance of a Lectureship in Secondary Education. To the study of problems in this field Professor Inglis devoted his professional career, leaving as a precious heritage to his co-workers the example of his industry, intellectual integrity, human sympathy, and social vision. It is the purpose of the Lectureship to perpetuate the spirit of his labors and contribute to the solution of problems in the field of his interest. The lectures on this foundation are published annually by the School.

FOREWORD

I AM often asked "What does Teachers College think about so and so?" The truthful answer is that the College, as an institution, holds no position, advocates no theory of education. It selects its faculty and, as every such institution must, permits each member untrammeled to present whatever his reflections and his researches lead him to believe. Harvard University is similarly liberal. It has invited me to deliver a lecture to commemorate Alexander Inglis, that lamented scholar, teacher, and friend, making no inquiries as to what I shall say and imposing no restrictions. If any parts of my address prove unpopular, the blame is mine — and mine alone.

The fundamental thesis that is developed is believed to be irrefutable; the implications in it are numerous and important. The philosophy may shock both the sentimental and the complacent — the former because it seems crass if one is satisfied by an illogical and unreasoned fetish, the latter because it is at once apparent that acceptance of the principle will necessitate material and far-reaching changes. Any frank speaking that disturbs conventional practice, especially if that practice has emotional rather than carefully reasoned intellectual approval, is likely to stir up resentment. The matter of the address is presented to the reason. If the positions taken are not sound, they should be refuted by facts and dispassioned arguments. Any discussion of them must begin and end with the fundamental thesis; any critic of competent and controlled intellect will keep it in mind and argue from it, however he may feel about the implications that it seems to carry. I have tried to make clear not only the soundness of the fundamental thesis, but also its importance and the necessity of applying it both as a criterion of current practices and as a directive force for a new and sounder educational program.

THE GREAT INVESTMENT

SECONDARY EDUCATION IN A DEMOCRACY

IN no other phase of life — unless, perhaps, in that of social customs — are we so likely as in education to take common practices for granted. Uncritically we continue general procedures, improving the means of making them effective, regardless of the fact that the original reasons for their adoption may never have been sound or that conditions which made them possible or imperative may have so changed as to necessitate material modification or even outright rejection at the present time. "It would seem at times that the means achieved have really usurped the place of the hoped for end." As the law of inertia operates in education no less than in physics, it is the part of wisdom now and then to reflect on the main features of its program, to review historical causes, to inventory affecting and affected conditions, to apply accepted philosophy, and thus to ascertain the validity or the weakness of what "everybody accepts."

An idea, like a coin, when constantly used finally has its sharp edges worn smooth. Its original value may still be inherent, but it is seldom recognized. That the counter may again be a coin it needs to be reminted, to have all its edges and significant lines made sharp and meaningful. This process reveals the counterfeit and the genuine. When we find the metal unalloyed and of full weight, a restamping reveals to all its value. It may then be used even with the stranger who might have rejected the worn counter as meaningless and valueless.

One of common practices in education that we propose for examination is that of free public education. In the United States it is a national ideal; no one questions it in principle. We pour forth taxes in large amounts that every one may have an opportunity at the expense of the State to acquire as much education as he may have the ambition and capacity to assimilate. Even more, we require by law that children attend school for increasing lengths of time, and we punish by fines and imprisonment adults who interfere. Free public schools are the boast of the orator, the satisfaction of the public, and the hope of the New World.

And yet free public education is relatively new in modern civilization. In Western Europe education was a private enterprise, extended by benevolence often to those who had no need of charity, until the French Revolution developed the idea of free elementary schools for all children. In our country they came late. It was only yesterday on the calendar of history that Barnard was arguing in Connecticut that the State should furnish free education for those who desired it. At first there was vigorous opposition from those who declared that the State might as well put its hand forcibly into their pockets to buy bread for other peoples' children as to give them schools; but the idea fell in with the theory of democracy and was made possible of application by the rapidly increasing wealth of the nation. Like a conflagration it spread throughout the country. Free elementary schools were established, supported, and improved. Laws were passed enforcing attendance, to protect children against exploitation and to insure them what finally came to be conceived as a "right." Later the idea was extended to include higher education, even on college and university levels. It comes as something of a surprise to many when they learn that our country is unique in this phase of its program. No other nation has ever in the history of the world extended the opportunities for free education so far or had them embraced by so many. The United States now enrolls a dozen times more of its adolescents in free public schools than even the progressive European countries enroll in advanced schools of all kinds, each of them charging fees to those who can pay, and strictly limiting admission to those of highly superior academic intelligences.

When we ask representative citizens, those who have paid their taxes and even been loyal supporters of the public schools, why the State should provide free education, it is revealed, oddly enough, that few have ever given so important a matter any thought whatever. Following are typical answers: "We've always provided free schools," which betrays ignorance of even recent history. "It's a good thing, and so I boost it," though how good is not specified in thought or in expression. "To make men free"; how? and for what? "The law requires it." "I've sometimes wondered, but never liked to oppose the majority," — that is, there was not enough strength to oppose inertia or the active force of those who have children to profit. "We have an obligation to pass on the inheritance of the ages," a statement that indicates no conception of how vast the intellectual inheritance is or of the necessity of a principle for selecting what fraction shall be selected for passing on at the expense of the State to any individual or group. "Every child in a democracy has a right to the development of his powers" or, as sometimes stated "to an even start in life." We naturally wonder if the loyal citizen thinks secondary education ever has given all children an even start;

and what is the sanction for the right to development of powers? Which powers? And to what extent?

That such answers are typical may be verified by any one who takes the trouble to propose the question to his friends and acquaintances. That they are insufficient is obvious. The sound basis of support in a democracy for any practice is an intelligent understanding and a consequently established faith. Traditional phrases and unanalyzed terms are shaky foundations when undermined by doubt and by the potent instruments of opposition. Despite the all but unanimous support that education has developed in public sentiment, there have of late been ominous questionings, which easily might so alarm the citizenry as to cause most disastrous results. Although the wealth of our country is abundantly able to spare what the schools cost, and more, for any approved cause, taxes are always onerous, especially in times of economic depression and when inequitable systems of taxation force on some a contribution heavier than they are willing to make. In an effort to reduce taxes, it is but natural that citizens look first at the largest single item; and that of course is the amount appropriated for schools. Varying widely in different communities, by and large it averages nearly half of every local budget. The size of this fraction makes it susceptible to attack; and when attacked it can be permanently supported and increased only if its justification and need are generally understood.

Questions are being increasingly raised, too, by parents and by pupils, who are paying far more than the State to this great experiment of extended general education. The latter devote years of their lives and much labor to tasks that are not always to them manifestly of value. In the great majority of cases parents have been and are willing to make sacrifices, often heroic sacrifices, that their children may have advantages which will advance them toward success; but questions are more and more frequently heard as to the results of the sacrifices. Parents stint themselves and the rest of the family that certain children may attend high school and college. They reasonably expect that the results will be so happy as to reveal a manifest justification of all that they have foregone. When they do not see in their children obvious advancement on a more prosperous and perfect life, and especially when, on inquiry, they can not be made to understand how the program of studies is expected to contribute in this direction for all students, very naturally they lose enthusiasm for universal education at the State's expense. Even if they do not have the vigor and courage to become active opponents, they become receptive of hostile criticism and ready to follow those who may lead opposition. Especially if they have no more children to send to school, they can find an outlet for their feelings chiefly through hostility to the mounting cost of public education. As the number of such disillusioned parents increases, the need of a clear understanding of the principle on which free public education is based is emphasized. Even if such parents do not actively express themselves in opposition to extended public education, the obligation of school officers to justify expenditures and to build a firm foundation of informed public intelligence is just as great.

Certainly "not just any kind" of education is justifiable. The theory on which public expenditure for free and even compulsory schools is developed should reasonably be expected to give direction to the kind of education that is provided and to determine the extent to which it is offered or compelled. Obviously it is impossible in this day and time for any one to acquire more than a small fraction of the inheritance of the ages. Even Aristotle could not compass it all in the distant day of Greece; and the inheritance is inestimably richer now. Selection must inevitably be made, and no such opinions as have been quoted from representative citizens give any suggestion of criteria for selection or for determining when the public obligation is satisfied. Education is too important, too potent for good, for both the individual and for the State, to be predicated on such perilous opinions. For its continuance, expansion, and direction a sounder basis should be generally known.

I

AFTER considering all the answers that have been proposed, by laymen on various levels and by the few professional educators who apparently have thought of the important matter, one on reflection finds that the reason why the State institutes schools, enforces attendance through the elementary stages, and makes no charge for tuition is absurdly simple. The State supports free public schools to perpetuate itself and to promote its own interests. Education is, then, a long-term investment that the State may be a better place in which to live and a better place in which to make a living.

This reason is so obviously sound and so obviously superior to all others that have been proposed that it apparently needs only understanding to gain approval. It would seem that some such reason must from early days have been in the popular mind, certainly that it must clearly be there now, to explain the practically unanimous support of public schools. Often there is disagreement in a community as to how much money shall be voted for their support, but it has been a long time since any one raised a voice against them as a justifiable institution. Every year to support free schools the State takes money from the purses of all of its citizens — from childless spinsters and bachelors, from retired farmers and bankers, and from "soulless corporations" as well as from parents. It never asks if the taxpayer "loves little children"; it never asks if he is willing to contribute; and strangely enough he never protests the principle. The question of public support for schools is settled and, whether understandingly or not, settled in the right way.

The reason is not only sound, it is also important. Already we are aware of a reaction to the rapid increase in the costs of public schools, a reaction which unless checked promises more seriously to cripple progress than it has already done in some communities. The only reliable way of insuring the continuance of generous support and of increasing it to an extent commensurate with estimated needs is to place it on a sound basis of reason. Free education is a business investment and not a benevolence.

Philanthropy, charitableness, and good will are welcomed as enriching educational support and opportunities; but reason is essential to insure justice and wise development. If education is seen as a necessity for preserving and for bettering the State, opposition to adequate appropriations takes on the tone of treason. The thesis that is being presented is no mere academic justification of the marvelous phenomenon of free public education in our country. It has many important implications, some of which will presently be discussed. To the extent to which it is understood and accepted it will give direction to reforms in education which in their perfection would be revolutionary.

Other forms of government may maintain themselves and even temporarily prosper with education limited to the few who direct and drive a vulgar populace; but in a democracy, where one vote counts for as much as another, where success is dependent upon unit citizens all sufficiently intelligent and informed and trained to evaluate and act wisely on their information, popular education is imperative. This statement needs no defense, so generally is it accepted. "A widespread righteousness is in a republic a matter of necessity. Where all rule all, each man who falls into evil courses infects his neighbor, corrupting the law and corrupting still more its enforcement. The question of manufacturing moral men becomes, accordingly, in a democracy, urgent to a degree unknown in a country where but a few selected persons guide the state." *

In other forms of government a leader is strong in proportion to the ignorance and the faith of his followers; democratic leadership is strong in proportion to the educated intelligence of the people. Carlyle once said, "Invent the printing press and democracy is inevitable." The printing press has long been invented — and many other causes of democracy; they have had their inevitable results, which are not likely for a long time to come, if ever, to be directed backward. Those who decry democracy and rejoice to point out its failures have not yet been able to propose anything approaching a satisfactory substitute. "The very ignorance, bias, frivolity, jealousy, instability, which are alleged to incapacitate them (the masses) from share in political affairs," says Dewey.† "unfit them still more for passive submission to rule by intellectuals." Whether democracy is in any degrees whatever good or bad, it is our accepted principle of government, and it can be made better only by an intelligently and purposefully directed

* Palmer, George Herbert: The Teacher, page 32.
† The Public and Its Problems, page 205.

education. The cure for democracy is truly more democracy — of a real kind. We are as a people fond of declaiming of liberty, but it is possible and can exist only through an education appropriate to each so that all have a chance to develop toward that element of equality without which the apotheosis of liberty can not exist.

The open questions are what kinds of education shall be provided and how far shall it extend. Fundamentally it must provide for such training as will perpetuate the State and promote its interests; and in wisdom it should continue until the law of diminishing returns begins to operate for each individual. Democracy is not "a utopia of escape," but a concatenation of opportunities for service. It can succeed only as this fact is perceived and as education is provided that sets up the proper attitude in young citizens and prepares them for such services to the State, indirect as well as direct, as each is competent to perform. De Tocqueville long ago pointed out "that popular government is educative as other modes of political regulation are not." Preparation of all for this type of higher assured and continuous education is more important in State supported schools than is preparation for the higher and for the great majority of secondary school students not sincerely desired college education, to which so much effort is now devoted. An appreciation of the imperative need of this kind of "preparatory schooling" will come only if the true function of State support of free schools is understood. Lest there be a misunderstanding, it should be clearly stated here that preparation for higher education, academic and technical, and provision of such education for those who have proved their competence for it are also an obligation of the State,* for such students thus trained will pay large dividends. But this preparation will, by the criterion implied, be limited and also supplementary to the preparation for the higher education that democracy demands and to an extent insures.

The activities undertaken by the State should be, and usually are, those affecting large numbers, usually all, of the population. In the case

* Throughout this discussion the term *State*, when capitalized, is used to indicate not political units of government, like Massachusetts or Arizona or North Carolina, but, rather, the societal organization that has assumed responsibility for education. It may be a local school district, a municipality, a county, a political state, the entire population of the country, or any combination of these. The tendency properly seems to be units of support of increasing extent, which is a recognition of the break-down with the developments in modern civilization of isolation and independence. This arbitrary definition must be kept continuously in mind when considering the arguments for the thesis herein defended.

of education the activities are intended primarily to modify and to improve the conduct of the pupils; but secondarily, and of far more importance, they will, or at least should, result in a contribution through improved conduct to all society with which the individuals come into relations, and these relations are not all by any means voluntarily chosen. One may within limits select his mate, his friends, and to a less extent his neighbors; but the members of larger societies are forced upon him by circumstances beyond his control. They affect his health, his prosperity, and his happiness no less truly than those with whom he has by his own volition elected to associate. Inasmuch as individuals do inevitably affect others, both directly and indirectly, affect them for good or for ill, society is concerned that each boy and girl be elevated to the highest plane of which he is capable. The chief means of such elevation is, of course, education; consequently society, or the State, as the term is here used, organizes and supports schools and even enforces attendance in order that it may protect itself and promote its own interests. This concept is of greater importance than at first it appears, because it leads to the inevitable conclusion that the State must, to protect its investment and to insure dividends on it, be concerned that the curriculum be formulated and

administered primarily with this end in view.
Lacking omniscience and consequent certainty
as to the exact goods which are desired, the State
may for the time being be liberal in its prescrip-
tions; but no less for this uncertainty does it
have the obligation to plan as wisely as possible
— and always in the direction of its own perpetuation and betterment.

It is not within the scope of this essay to indicate all the details in which education is essential to the perpetuation and the promotion of the
government which we have accepted or, even if
wisdom were possessed, of enumerating at this
time the means that a popular educative program
should use to achieve its ends. The hope here
is that turning attention to the reason why free
education is supported by the State and presenting a reasonable justification of it will result in
an understanding by the public, led by its professional experts, of the necessity of developing an educative program that promises achievement of the desired ends. Surely among other
objectives a curriculum devised to perpetuate
and to improve the State would lead to a better
understanding by the next generations of the
ideals of democratic living, social as well as
political, — an understanding not only of the
ideals but of their justifications and of the necessity for their approximation in living. Thus

there would result a far better knowledge than now exists or has ever existed in the past of the rules of the game essential for happy and prosperous living, and a better disposition to follow them.

Laws are broken largely because of selfishness, and selfishness is in chief measure due to a lack of knowledge and imagination of remote and important consequences. All proposals for the reduction in the number of violations of the law are of petty significance when contrasted with the one means that can be effective. That means is education devised in consonance with the thesis under discussion. Knowledge of such facts and principles as are ordinarily taught may be involved in the prevention, but they are not sufficient. Remedies for the amelioration of conditions disturbing thoughtful leaders are doubtless possible and desirable; but inevitably we are forced to conclude that the only means that will materially improve the observance of and respect for laws, which are or should be society's rules of the game of happy and prosperous living, are an education that for the good of the supporting State will lead to an understanding of the reasons for such laws and of the large and ultimate consequences of their observation and of their violation. This is but one of the many objectives that the new curriculum devised to insure dividends on the long-term investment by the State in education will of necessity set up. When once the principle is understood and accepted by the public, the ingenuity of professional schoolmen, properly supported by an informed citizenry, can invent and administer a detailed program quite as successfully as they have done for less definite and less justifiable ends.

There are four means that the State chiefly uses or can use to insure its perpetuation: war, the police force, social pressure, and education. The first two, being concretely obvious and effective of immediate results, are generally recognized and on necessity supported with all requisite assets. But is there any wisdom in the costly expediency of war without provision for an education which is directed to prevent its recurrence? Is there any wisdom in outpouring a large fraction of the material wealth of a nation and in sacrificing a considerable fraction of its essential capital, the lives of its citizens, to preserve the State from outside enemies when the greater danger from internal disease is ignored? Is any wisdom in continuing the palliation by police power, the covering up of sores, while neglecting the prevention of the internal condition of which they are merely symptoms? War is not merely the mobilization and use of force. Its stern and vital challenge turns the emphasis as the gentler but no less vital challenge of peace never yet has done to the importance of education. War can not be waged by a democracy until the citizens are educated to believe in its necessity; it can not be effective until its citizens are educated to do with actual, not hoped for, satisfaction the tasks assigned them. There has never yet been in the minds of a public any equivalent for war in revealing the mutual dependence of a citizenry, the necessity of integration into social solidarity, and the importance of education that is directed toward clearly formulated objectives and that actually produces what it sets out to obtain.

And yet, the challenge in peace to build up the State weakened by war, to change neutral or even hostile citizens into strong supporters and active followers of approved practices, to develop and encourage the able to propose and to promote improvements that will make for general health and strength — this challenge, though less obvious and less dramatic, is no less real and no less important. A soldier who in four months or in four minutes lays down his life to preserve the State is more spectacular but no less patriotic than the teacher who for forty years contributes his strength, genius, patience, and industry to promote as well as to preserve that which makes happy and prosperous living possible. But the teacher who for hire doles out details selected, assembled, and arranged by others without appreciation of their societal significance and without whole-hearted devotion to the opportunity for service in making the State a better place in which to live and a better place in which to make a living can claim no more importance in this world's affairs than the uninterested retailer of any other prepared commodity. Both are working merely to preserve their own self-centered lives — the latter frankly, the former hypocritically under the guise of "service."

It is strange that from Colonial times to the present there should have been so clear and general an understanding that war is essential to preserve the larger State and that after its conclusion so few should have realized the necessity of education for continuing its preservation and also of promoting its interests. Our Colonial ancestors fought to rid themselves of tyranny, to make a nation possible; they published bills of rights, they loosened the restricting bonds, they set up a constitution, and then sat back to await the millennium of liberty. How much they might have accelerated its coming, for which we still await, had they intelligently used education to prepare future citizens for their privileges and their obligations. In the

Civil War after narrowly escaping wreck on the shoals of division, the Federal government freed millions of slaves, accepted them into citizenship, and conferred on them the suffrage. Did it follow up its preservation of a weakened State and its substitution of a people inferior because of ignorance for the fallen superior citizens by an intelligent program of effecting through education a real union and of fitting through education the youth of the land as well as the newly enfranchised horde for an understanding of the State and for attitudes as well as skills that would promote its interests and make it a better place in which to live and in which to make a living? It did not. The great opportunity lost, the wounded State struggled painfully and slowly back to an undirected unity, which because of natural resources, a vigorous people, and the grace of God has reached its present effectiveness. One is appalled to see how the State has poured out its money to establish schools in which for a long time even the teaching of civic duties was neglected and in which for many years — and to some extent even now — were permitted histories that kept old sores open and sensitive and that conspicuously failed to unify a people in the principles on which the State rests. During the World War the Committee on Public Information was active and notably successful in unifying our people through education concerning the reasons for the war, its progress, its purposes, and the means by which every one could help. We were instructed — and in a large measure successfully — that we were fighting and sacrificing and suffering "to make the world safe for democracy." But immediately that the armistice was signed the Committee on Public Information was dispersed, and no generally directed activity to teach what democracy is and what its privileges, implications, and obligations are was instituted to take its place. It is as truly essential to perpetuate the State in peace as to preserve it in war, and at all times it is wise to use every possible agency to seek its improvement.

The police force is maintained to preserve the State through preventing those violations of the rules which we have agreed are necessary to restrain those whose ignorance, narrow vision, or selfish impulses would act contrary to the general good. Almost always the police force is negative in its effects; it restrains but it seldom promotes. Social pressure is even more effective, restraining and also promoting: one can not live amicably with his neighbors when he does not play the game according to the rules, whether officially adopted or not, that they set up. On a moment's thought it will be realized that social pressure is the result of education of some sort, in the home, in the church, from pulpit and platform, through the press, from incidental contacts in work or play, in clubs and societies, or in the formal schools. The only agency that the State controls and therefore can assuredly use for perpetuating its ideals and for directing its citizens to better living is, of course, the schools. In the discussion of war it may have seemed that emphasis was laid entirely on the political state, but that is only one phase. There are others of even greater importance, which the political state is maintained merely to make possible. Everything is involved that makes the community a better place in which to live and a better place in which to make a living.

It must not be thought that the formal schools have done nothing to preserve the State and to promote its interests. They have done a great deal; indeed, it may safely be maintained that no other agency has done so much. Their direct influence is great; their indirect is greater still. An examination of textbooks, especially of those in literature, civics, and history, will reveal how deeply the several authors are concerned with inculcating not only knowledge but also ideals that should — and doubtless reasonably do — affect living. Even in unsuspected subjects, such as philology and geography, as Carleton Hayes has deprecatingly pointed out, nationalism is developed. But it is in extra curricula activities that the secondary schools are now most effective — not only in the clubs, assemblies, and the like, but also in the more or less intimate personal contacts of teachers with students, which increasingly are provided for by instituting home-rooms and providing advisers. The effects of all this formal and informal teaching by the schools are unquestionably direct and great in the later as well as in the immediate attitudes and actions of the students; indirectly they to a considerable extent doubtless influence what the alumni pass on as parents, neighbors, editors, promoters, and priests.

The greater the effects, the more concern the State has with what the schools teach. Genuine education is dangerous, for it leads to positive action affecting the social body. Conversely it may be maintained that when education is not dangerous, when it merely presents, however skilfully, innocuous facts, however highly organized, it is not important. The fact that the schools do attempt, by formal and by informal means, to influence the attitudes and the actions of their students immediately and later when they are full-fledged citizens is no evidence that they do their job wisely or that they accomplish anything like maximum results. Except sporadically and usually in superficial matters the State has not been concerned with what effects the schools have on making each community a better place in which to live and a better place in which to make a living. As it pays the bills it has a right to be; as its prosperity, to say nothing of its very life, is dependent on the results, it has an obligation to be.

From the earliest days there have been high declarations of the purposes of education. But we have done precious little to insure that dividends of the kind desired are paid on the investment. We have largely left the decision as to what shall be taught in matters essential to the State's welfare to individual teachers or to small groups who have either not been aware of the larger obligations of public education or have blandly ignored them.

It is true that there has been passed much legislation concerning the curriculum, but it has usually grown out of the efforts of active minorities who have promoted some phase of instruction without a conception of the large functions of education or a vision of the whole problem. The curriculum is too important and too complex to be determined even in part by laymen, especially by those who are so devoted to single and often selfish phases that they can not see the problem as a whole. Similarly the curriculum is too important and too complex to be determined by professional schoolmen unless they base it on principles which are approved by the State and which are consistently applied in the discovery and organization of details. It is difficult to give this matter the emphasis that its importance warrants.

At the risk of seemingly tedious repetitions, we must again assert that education is the sole means that the State has for presenting such knowledge and of inculcating such attitudes as are necessary for maintaining the approved standards of living and of raising them toward higher ideals. Just any knowledge is not sufficient; the choice, especially the omissions, organization, and interpretation, when left to those only partly competent may even make against the good of the supporting State. Certainly the highest and best dividends can not be expected unless all the intelligence of society contributes to the formulation. It is a problem for the whole people, who must insure that their experts begin with a satisfactory philosophy and who must supply them, as has never up to this time been done, with adequate machinery for the necessary research.

A sound curriculum can not be expected from the efforts of teachers undertaking revision as a task additional to their normal duties, from small groups who lack data that can be provided only by extensive and expensive research and who are not soundly based on the understanding and philosophy that are necessary to give direction; nor can it be expected from individuals or small groups who are interested to develop some minor phase regardless of the whole pattern. Society must appropriate as generously for its school curriculum as industry does to develop its processes — and that means millions to be spent by the best minds uninterruptedly devoting themselves to the continuous and never-ending task.

Recently we have noted a flare-up of public sentiment in protest against proposed use of the schools to inculcate information and attitudes, which if unhindered would doubtless have eventuated in action of some importance affecting public welfare. A powerful combination of corporations proposed units of instruction, for which it promised to furnish free materials, which were calculated to influence the coming generation of voters favorably to their business. The protest of the intelligensia and of publicists generally was immediate, vigorous, and effective. There is little doubt that the general public would have reacted similarly, had it been informed of the proposed propaganda. And yet, having prevented the introduction of units of instruction which the corporations were wise enough to see would influence sentiment in a way profitable to them, the public, or its spokesmen, subsided, leaving the schools to teach in the important matter of utilities pretty much what they please, pretty much in the ways that they please. Sensitive to resent and to defeat the efforts of a minority to use education for selfish ends, it was not sagacious enough to recognize the opportunity, the need, and the obligation to use education for the perpetuation and the promotion of the ideals and principles that control and direct the State in which we must all find our welfare and our happiness. Negativism is not sufficient. A positive program is imperative. If our State, as previously defined, is good, we must be concerned actively to see that youth is instructed in such ways that it is continued and improved. There are always weaknesses of mankind and selfishness of individuals and small groups that are making against general happiness and general prosperity.

When such matters are discussed the emotions are easily involved to such an extent that the main issue is beclouded and there are raised numerous apparent objections. These should be discussed — they probably have all been considered — if there were time or if less reflective readers were addressed. One objection has so frequently been introduced into informal discussion of the thesis that it deserves some answer here. Emphasis on the right and the obligation of the State to use publicly supported education for the maintenance of accepted social and economic theories often calls forth the rejoinder that the schools are to maintain the *status quo,* stifle independent thinking, and prevent progress. To a certain extent, to a very small extent, this is true. It would be disastrous if the general *status quo* were constantly attacked or were suddenly changed, especially before a better program is soundly developed. No public philosophy that works as well as ours has worked can be altogether bad. Or, to state it positively, our program of life is largely good, better in the judgment of the vast majority than any substitute proposed by radicals or by reactionaries. The State, as argued, supports education primarily as a gigantic balance wheel precisely to impart information and to inculcate attitudes such as will keep the machinery running without disturbing friction and disastrous consequences. Defects there are, to be sure, but until adult society has decided how they should be remedied surely it is not thinkable that children and immature youth should be given over to any individual or small group of individuals whose panaceas have not been able to win the approval of the matured public. Certainly the elementary and secondary schools are not the instruments to revolutionize the State. As soon as an improvement of any kind is accepted by the public, then it becomes a part of the State program and is therefore properly a matter of instruction.

In so far as the objection argues that our postulate stifles independent thinking and thus prevents progress, it is sound only for a poor kind of education, the kind that has often been permitted because the possible potency of a better kind was not realized. Unquestionably much education, in our country as in others, in our time as in the past, has stifled thought; unquestionably it is having that disastrous result now and will have it in the future. Why? Because the public has not been sufficiently concerned with the essentials of education, because it has not demanded that it pay dividends of the best kind to the State. While providing generously for buildings and other physical appurtenances, it has permitted those of limited competence to frame the curriculum, to impart its content, and to exert those irregular and intangible influences which are perhaps even more important. School people are limited in competence not so much in the details of their jobs as in a large comprehension of their significance. In other words, like the lay public they need more than anything else an understanding of what education is for, of the ends that it is supported to achieve. Thought may be stifled so that either beneficent or maleficent immediate conclusions are reached, but in either case the results must ultimately be bad.

It is often said that the schools should teach how to think rather than what to think. From such an ideal no one can dissent. Lay critics often assume that when they have enunciated such a principle they are taking issue with educators. But indeed they are not. Hardly a treatise on education but has argued for the same ideal; scarcely a teacher but writes it as Article One of the professional creed. But the practical challenge of the classroom reveals to the teacher, as reflection should reveal to any intelligent layman, that the how and the what are inextricably interwoven. The best teachers — in the formal school, in the home, or on the platform — may aim at the ideal of independent thinking; but at the same time they profoundly influence thinking toward results that they have accepted. This is due largely, of course, to the fact that such thinking as they themselves have done, thinking which they correctly or incorrectly consider independent, has led them to conclusions which seem sound; and immature minds are easily influenced to follow the same patterns to similar results. The practical situation, especially in the pressure to instruct large classes, reveals, too, the wide differences in and the severe limitations to independent thinking. Teachers seek to secure the ideal and measurably succeed; but after all their efforts perhaps the majority of units of instruction teach and will continue to teach more of the what than of the how. Approving the ideal, we must admit this fact. If the State decides that better training in powers of independent thinking is essential for its welfare, it must provide better machinery, primarily extensive and expensive researches as to method, for the achievement of that end. In the meantime it is concerned with what is taught. In both matters the thesis under consideration will furnish the fundamental criterion. What students are taught to think and how they are taught to think should contribute to the perpetuation and to the improvement of the State.

When formulating its educational ideals a democratic State would unquestionably emphasize instruction in how to think. Thus it would attempt to develop leaders on various levels and in all independence that will support, check, and direct those chosen for responsibility. But as thinking is never done in a vacuum, instruction will always involve facts, their interpretation, and their relations, and involving them it will for all students in some degree, and for the less gifted predominantly, also teach what to think. Admitting this fact, the State is faced with the alternative, on the one hand, of devising a curriculum that attempts to support the highest approved philosophy or, on the other, of leaving to individuals or to small and irresponsible groups of individuals the formulation of a curriculum that promotes other and perhaps deleterious conceptions of life.

When such an alternative is frankly faced, it is inconceivable that the State should provide and maintain a costly system of schools and that it should supply its most precious possession, the embryos of the new society, and then leave the direction of their destiny to chance, to selfish interests, or to less than the maximum organization of the best wisdom that exists for societal good. It is inconceivable, but this is precisely what the State has to the largest extent done. Why? Partly because in rapid growth it has been concerned primarily with providing the means for education; partly because in its vigorous young manhood with its exuberance of strength and vitality it has not felt the need; partly because it has never fully and frankly faced the issue; and partly because it has not yet found itself, has not yet clarified its vision of what the democratic life is and what it desires.

That the results have been no worse is due to the common sense and the integrity of those men and women who have led and served, however humbly, in developing the congeries, rather than a system, of schools. Their understanding of democracy may have been partial, but on the whole it is sincere; their evaluation of propaganda has not been perfect, but it has generally been in the direction of wisdom; and their interpretation of what they have inherited and of what they have invented as a curriculum has by and large made for good. That the results may be better, that proper and possible dividends may be assured on the largest investment that society has made, the State must realize why it supports education, why it makes it free, why it passes laws for compulsory attendance; and then it will as seriously provide machinery for making a curriculum that will insure its perpetuation and improvement as it now provides for good buildings or roads or any other physical thing.

From the illustrations used it may be concluded by some who do not carefully read that there is an implied argument for determining the school program by popular vote. Nothing could be more absurd. For its own interests the State has other departments than education, such, for example, as that of health. Over each one it places selected experts, whose training and experience are trusted to determine the program that shall be followed. But the very selection of an expert, by the public as well as by an individual, to some extent involves an expression of opinion or judgment: for example, the head of a board of health may be chosen from the allopaths, the homeopaths, or the Christian Scientists. Through their directors the stockholders of a corporation in selecting an expert to manage their properties consider his training, his experience, and his personality (which often means his philosophy); they consider and approve, after possible amendment, his general program, and then, if they are wise, they furnish the necessities and leave to him the details of administration. The expert may recommend that a mill be changed so as to manufacture gray goods rather than cotton prints, or rayon rather than ginghams; decision on such a matter is the prerogative of the stockholders. When it is made, the expert manager is left to work out the details and is held responsible for production and for dividends.

The analogy is close enough to indicate what is argued for education. The public as a whole are the stockholders providing the capital and profiting or losing by the investment. Those who furnish the raw material, in this case the children, have only as stockholders rather than as parents a voice in the kinds of products that shall be sought by the schools. If the stockholders through their directors decide that they wish boys and girls turned out with developed powers of independent thinking, of making a living, of performing the duties of citizenship, or of doing any other thing whatever, that is their prerogative. They should then select as manager someone who by training, experience, and philosophy is considered competent to produce what is wanted. To him will be left decision as to details. He may report that if product X is wanted he must have funds for research which will show how it may be obtained — economically or at all, — or that he must have extensive new machinery, or better operatives. The stockholders may in any case decide that the cost is too great to warrant the outlay or they may be convinced that it seems a good investment and so make the necessary appropriations. In any case, the expert is held responsible for dividends. It is not sufficient for him to blame the operatives, to find fault with the raw materials, to submit that he has done the best that he could. If dividends are not forthcoming, new machinery is provided, better operatives are secured, the management is changed, or decision is made that a different kind of product shall be sought. In this great investment of popular education two factors are constant: the stockholders and the raw materials. The supporting State, be it large or small, maintains schools for its perpetuation and improvement; these ends are attainable through the betterment of the children of the community, whatever their natural abilities, aptitudes, or interests.

This is a principle fundamental for all to understand who undertake the direction of public education, either as interested stockholders or as professional experts. In no other important and highly technical matter have individuals of the lay public assumed so much knowledge or arrogated to themselves such powers of suggestion and interference. This is chiefly due to the fact that every one through his experiences in schools has ideas, often sound and important, sometimes silly and trivial because of *ad hominem* arguments; but in no small degree it is also due to the fact that experts in education are relatively few among teachers and even among administrators, and that often those who are qualified to be most expert make decisions and pursue policies on grounds where the lay public are equally competent to stand. There is no true expertness except that based upon sound pragmatic principles and upon carefully ascertained facts. Whenever the professional expert speaks in his own person, relying merely on greater experience or on authority of elected position, rather than on approved principles and verified facts, that moment he ceases to be expert and lays himself open to attack by others who apply the criteria of limited experience and common sense. It is the function of the expert, so far as it is possible, to explain his principles, to adduce his facts, and to gain approval by the public of his general program. By this policy he has an impregnable position. Mistakes he may make in administrative or teaching details, but they are and can be shown to be relatively unimportant in the general scheme, if that is understood and approved as wise. The public will follow and support him not because of the attribution of occult insight, but because they realize the soundness of the program for the creation of desired dividends; and in their appreciation of economy in the distribution of labor they will yield personal preferences based on admittedly limited experience to the recondite facts which in his training he has found.

There has certainly been much mischievous meddling by the public in school affairs, but its solicitude with what education seeks to do and with what it actually accomplishes has been too occasional, too slight, and too much concerned with trivial and personal details. It can safely be asserted that the public is too little informed and too little active in approving the essentials of the school program and far too lax in auditing the books to see that the desired dividends are abundantly paid on the greatest investment that can be made. The reluctance of the public to vote for increased expenditures is due not to poverty or to niggardliness, as is often charged, but rather to their ignorance of exactly what the schools are attempting to achieve and of their accomplishments in terms of a better State. Just as philosophy, according to his statement, taught Aristotle to accept willingly what other men had to accept protestingly, so an understanding of this fundamental philosophy of education and appreciation of the results of boys and girls better able and better disposed to contribute to the betterment of the State will assuredly bring the generous, enthusiastic, and wise support that is necessary.

It is postulated that education will make any community a better place in which to live. A mere enumeration of the stated objectives of education as they affect conduct and character, with analysis of some of the more general terms, will reveal how ambitious and how benevolent its program is and, in accordance with the vision of each generation, always has been. One may safely prophesy that in proportion to its enlightenment every people in every time will continue to profess its faith in education to influence its youth toward a higher life. To make our case it is unnecessary to assume that the objectives are perfect; they merely reflect ideals that stir in the bosoms of the people and are expressed by their leaders. Nor is it necessary to assume perfection of attainment in the inculcation of all the virtues which it has been proposed to seek. Any reasonable achievement of the professed goals and any consequent practice of the approved virtues by citizens must make a community an attractive place for other men and women desirous of the good life and must make its achievement easier to approximate.

An educated community insures a comfortable degree of integration on respectable and enduring levels. Those who have profited by education know many things in common, think much in common, and have in common many feelings about right and beauty that enable them to live together in amity and without embarrassing ignorance and misunderstanding. They find congeniality in so many phases of life that a true society results. They can appreciate and show tolerance to those who for one reason or another differ in their interests, attitudes, and conduct, especially to those whose independent thinking leads them onward to challenging departures from common practices.

But as "progress does not depend upon the similarity which we *find* but upon the similarity which we *achieve*,"* education carries the responsibility for the largest part of the increase of desirable integration. A State is sovereign, wrote Viscount Haldane, "in so far as its members in unity direct themselves in the expression of the common purposes they are evolving. . . . It gives rise to the power of a great group unified by common ends."

The educated furnish stimulus to growth, which is the most satisfying of all man's activities, because the truly educated never cease themselves to grow. They are fecund of a variety of means to meet the problems of life, proposing this means and that until a solution is found that profits all the members of the larger social group. This ability in even a single individual makes a community a better place in which to live; when possessed by all, or even by many, it becomes a tremendously profitable social asset. The educated, too, are in varying degrees rich in resources for avocational and for vocational successes. As time never hangs heavy on their hands, they escape many of the temptations of less fortunate people to meddle and to interfere with the affairs of others; instead, they are ready to share their wealth of

* Follett, The New State.

ideas and tastes with those who have a measure of appreciation. They furnish to others desires and emulations to increase their intellectual, æsthetic, and moral resources, that life may be more abundant and that they may share it more generously with others in their social groups.

The educated make a community a better place in which to live, further, because their own appetites, desires, and demands have brought together the means of satisfying numerous and various wants. Among them are libraries, museums, exhibits of art in its many forms, from painting and sculpture through architecture and a well-planned city, parks for recreation, places of entertainment on the levels sufficiently high that they demand effort for enjoyment and result in a satisfying consciousness of growth, conveniences of every kind, skilled service for all needs. The variety and richness of such assets, all of which have come because of educated needs, attract new citizens and make all comfortable to whatever extent they are used. The poorest inhabitant of such a community has an actual as well as a potential wealth greater than any one can possess in a community which has not been built up by demands of those made competent by education.

Partly because of education, partly because

of its results, and partly, perhaps, because of other reasons, communities rank as to poverty and crime inversely on the whole as they rank in education. There is strong reason for believing that the negative correlation would be even larger still if the machinery of education were directed more consistently and more intelligently toward achieving economic comforts and respect for law, whether common or statute, objectives that are generally proclaimed and commonly neglected in practice. Similarly, education contributes somewhat and indubitably could contribute much more to making communities better in which to live by raising the levels on which intelligence commonly operates, especially regarding matters of wide social concern and specifically of political action. Obviously a democratic government is not successful unless the voices of the people are raised for and against proposals according to social values; and obviously the more informed the citizens are, the more skilfully they use native intellectual gifts in perceiving the better among the worse, just so much more successful democracy will be. If education can not, when it seriously wills to do so, affect such matters, what agency, pray, can be trusted to influence the people consistently for the common good? When ignorance, prejudices, and short-sightedness — and it is these

far more often than malevolence — commonly
lead to votes that negate those supported by the
opposite characteristics, no government is on a
sound foundation; it can not continue to make
its territory a better place in which to live. Any
one who permits himself to think on this matter
must realize the direct dependence of democracy
on education — not an education that is merely
memoriter fact accumulations, but one that is
seriously concerned with preserving the State
and with bettering it in every way possible.

And finally to be mentioned, though doubtless
there are other contributions, education tends to
make any community a better place in which to
live by raising the standards of living. This in
many ways it assuredly does. It affords some
direct instruction, which it might easily increase
in amount and in effectiveness; it reveals both in
its plant and through instruction higher types
than many pupils know; it employs teachers who
by various means have learned what higher
standards are and also the advantages of following them. A low standard of living by one
family is degrading to a neighborhood; seldom
concealed, it is infectious. A high standard, on
the other hand, is an example, an encouragement,
and a stimulus to emulation. It can not be
doubted that education has greatly affected standards of living or that it can be made to do more.

The extent to which education helps to a higher standard is an important contribution to making the whole community a better place in which all may live.

It is argued, too, that education makes a community better in which to earn a living. Of course a very small part of the curriculum has been formulated with the intent of directly contributing to economic effectiveness; and on the higher levels liberal and cultural courses may so divert interests and ambitions from economic accumulation that, after a comfortable living is assured, powers are directed to an enriched life with the result that earnings are below those which are possible. By all ideal standards this is entirely as it should be. As any one who has studied the various attempts to prove the economic values of education will realize, the problem is very complex. Often cause and effect are confused and a common cause for both education and prosperity is ignored. But the evidence, which there is no space to review here, seems unmistakable. There is a close relationship between such education as is provided and economic prosperity. The ability to read, to figure, to apply acquired knowledge, and to learn new processes more economically has contributed to make men better able to make a living. That the contribution of education to earning power could be considerably greater if curricula were made more directly vocational is so obvious as to need no argument.

The effect of general education on the ability to make a living, whatever its scientific explanation, is too commonly recognized to be entirely fallacious. The following quotation from Macaulay is illustrative:

"But by far the most important event of this short session was the passing of the Act for the settling of schools. By this memorable law it was, in the Scotch phrase, statuted and ordained that every parish in the realm should provide a commodious school house and should pay a moderate stipend to a schoolmaster. The effect could not be immediately felt. But, before one generation had passed away, it began to be evident that the common people of Scotland were superior in intelligence to the common people of any other country in Europe. To whatever land the Scotchman might wander, to whatever calling he might betake himself, in America or in India, in trade or in war, the advantage which he derived from his early training raised him above his competitors. If he was taken into a warehouse as a porter, he soon became foreman. If he enlisted in the army, he soon became a sergeant. Scotland, meanwhile, in spite of the barrenness of her soil and the severity of her climate, made such progress in agriculture, in manufactures, in commerce, in letters, in science, in all that constitutes civilization, as the Old World had never seen equalled, and as even the New World has scarcely seen surpassed." *

In our devotion to cultural education, the importance of which is not only conceded but emphasized, we often lose sight of the fact that it contributes to only one phase of the perfect man. No person can ideally be a good citizen unless he is equipped by nature and by training to make a living, and the more adequate that is, the better in many ways for his neighbors as well as for himself and his family. The ship of state can not move steadily or comfortably forward with a cargo of inactive and noncontributory passengers. Hence for the perpetuation and also for the promotion of the State, education should insure that every citizen be better prepared to make a better living for himself and for his dependents. As a matter of fact, almost every person does learn in some way to make a living. It is only reasonable to assume that by special instruction every one can be trained so that he can be made more quickly productive and also efficient on a higher level — both for making a living and for making a life. If such training, during the twelve to fifteen year period, could increase the

* Macaulay, History of England, Chapter XXII.

annual earning power by only ten per cent, which seems a modest expectancy, the increment of income would pay the entire cost of the public school system.

But it is not merely by increasing productiveness that education contributes to making the State a better place in which to make a living. Education of the consumer increases demands and thus furnishes work for others. Many shortsighted economists in their enthusiasm for the development of foreign markets for our goods lose sight of the fact that the best market, and ultimately the only one that can continue to pay for what it buys without disturbing exchange, is here at home. So as education has revealed the higher necessities of life, or the necessities of higher life, and has created a keen appetite for them, it has tended to make the State a better place in which to make a living. Where there are large demands there are opportunities for work, which in part explains the migration in our country from the rural to urban communities, for in spite of improved transportation it is in the cities that greater demands usually afford greater opportunities.

There is sufficient evidence to warrant our believing that education reduces crime and even more reason to make us confident that it could tremendously increase its influence in this respect if it seriously undertook the responsibility. The same evidence makes us believe that education has had no inconsiderable part in reducing poverty, in increasing the saving of what has been earned, not for hoarding but for intelligent investment for larger production. Certainly it would not be hard to prove that popular education has reduced disease, both by making every one aware of laws of health which he must follow and also hospitable to the advice and services of the expert, whom education has made an asset to the State. If education does decrease crime, poverty, and disease, it has very materially contributed to making the State a better place in which to make a living.

II

When the thesis that education should be considered as a long-term investment by the State that it may perpetuate itself and promote its own interests is proposed, there is a tendency toward accepting it as a harmless generality or an ineffective platitude. It is anything but that. Once accepted, it has implications that modify one's whole philosophy of education; it ramifies into attitudes and actions that are far from ineffective for any one who takes the trouble to think through the whole matter.

It follows, as a matter of course, that investments should pay dividends. What is desired from the investment of education is a citizenry made better able and better disposed to contribute to the betterment of the State. It follows that the whole educational program should be planned to that end, and that its success should be measured by the contributions made or likely to be made. At this point one may object that we do not know just what we want the State to be, revealing a need antecedent to a philosophy of education and fundamental to any program that can in any larger sense be satisfactory. It is true that there is no complete and generally understood concept of the good State, and because of this lack the State is to an extent weak. But there is a large corpus of generally agreed on details of the good State, and perhaps an even larger body of details that almost every one understands to be bad for effective living. Some of these ideals, both positive and negative, are incorporated into constitutions and statute laws; far more of them are a part of the mores, the folk ways of doing things, of good manners, of religion, as distinguished from theology, of common everyday living. To some extent they are passed on to each new generation informally and more or less fortuitously. If they are important (and who doubts that they are?) the State needs to insure

that each and every young citizen not only becomes aware of them, but accepts them as good
and learns how to translate them into actual
living. The only instrument that the State has
for effecting this desired and necessary end is
the schools.

Beyond the generally understood and approved ideals of the good State there are higher
and more comprehensive concepts in the minds of
specialists in government and in sociology. So
far as is possible, these should be simplified by
the expert leaders and when approved by the people or by their representatives they should be insured formal presentation, with interpretation
and practice in application, to each oncoming
wave of new generations. Again it will be seen
that the schools alone can perform this important
piece of work, with most probability of impartial
presentation that will reach every individual and
of skilled instruction that will result in understanding and in directed application for the beginning of habits.

Many of the simpler concepts of the good
State and some of those that are more complex
are passed on by other agencies, but never with
assurance that they will reach and be accepted by
all citizens, especially unadulterated and in the
form that is approved as most likely to be good.
The very fact that a considerable number of

citizens are not aware of many important principles in the philosophy of the good State and are not concerned with them as practical matters is a cogent reason why a program of education shall be formulated to correct the deficiency. If those concepts and principles are important for the integration of the citizens, for the perpetuation of the State, and for its promotion, there can not be permitted instruction that is biased, warped, or ineffective. Uncertainty as to the details does not impeach the thesis of education as a State investment. It merely emphasizes the necessity of using the schools for passing on what is accepted in order that the next steps may be taken toward advancement. Education will assuredly set up some sorts of ideals and attitudes. It is merely a question whether the representatives of the State will prepare a comprehensive program consistent with the best principles of social living, a program which will be presented uniformly throughout our country to all youth or, on the other hand, whether it will be left to individuals or to small groups, who may lack understanding, who may be out of sympathy with important details, who may present an incomplete and inconsistent theory — who may, in short, make the investment not only ineffective but positively harmful to the supporting State.

One objection is sure to be voiced when the thesis is presented that education is an investment by the State for the promotion of its own interests. That objection is based on concern for the rights of the individual and a fear that he may be prostituted by corporate society. Fortunately there is in reality little conflict. The interests of the State can be best served only if the individual is at the same time carefully developed in a way that is best for him. The State needs citizens effective in all sorts of ways — in commerce and in chemistry, in agriculture and in astronomy, in manufacture and in mathematics. The natural laws of competition and of demand ultimately thwart individual aspirations and hopes, which are usually confused with the so-called rights, far more than the State is likely to do.

The State can not be bettered unless the individual is first bettered himself, and so he is not likely to suffer under the principle that is being defended. But unfortunately it often appears to a short-sighted vision that the individual can be profited with no obvious or probable benefit to the supporting State. In such a situation there will be conflict. Let us suppose, for illustration, that a pupil has a desire to enter some college not for its academic training but for the pleasure that is possible in its social life or the prestige of being an alumnus. Let us suppose, further, that because of indolence or of inability he has shown during his introductory courses in mathematics no promise of even a reasonable success in pursuing the advanced courses necessary for admission. Which interests shall be dominant in a decision as to whether he shall be permitted to pursue advanced courses in the public secondary school? Shall those in authority, representing the State, use public funds for the further presentation of a subject that the pupil could not or would not in the past reasonably master so that it promised any material values to him? Does the objective that he seeks, a period of carefree comraderie, promise enough of value to him to make it reasonable to expect him thereby to be a better citizen? If a case can not be made for the further expenditure of public funds with a reasonable expectancy of profitable returns, responsibility rests with the pupil and his parents to secure at their own expense preparation for the desired end.

It may be objected further that the school authorities may be in error in their judgment or that the pupil may turn over a new leaf and manifest better results or that when he gets into college he may be awakened to keen academic interests. Such arguments would be considered absurd everywhere else in the world. School authorities may err in judgment, though naturally they should exercise every care possible not to do so and always are likely to give an individual the benefit of a doubt; but they have a responsibility to follow such judgments as they are able to make on the basis of accumulated evidence. If they err frequently and seriously, they are of course incompetent and should be replaced. It is the most patent dishonesty, of course, for one set in a position of trust by the State to shirk responsibility merely because it is personally unpleasant. It is possible that the pupil may make a new start and do better work; but if every reasonable effort has been unsuccessfully made to get good work in the preliminary courses, the responsibility now shifts to the pupil. If he manifests his ability and his willingness to work in other similar courses, which may be provided, or in the subject which he pursued under private instruction, the school authorities may properly reinstate him as a good investment, reasonably expecting profitable returns to the State that provides the funds. But the responsibility after failure is his. (There is, of course, some essential learning that must be imparted at any cost whatever, precisely because it is essential; but in the illustration that is being developed, this is not the case.) And, finally, it is possible that a student may after going to college with an unworthy motive awaken to the value of its courses and profit materially from them. It is possible, but what is the probability? Decision should be made here as in any other investment. If all knowledge of this student and of former students who have gone forward under similar circumstances makes the risk a reasonable one, the school authorities will take it — primarily, however, because success will make the investment profitable to the State through the betterment of the individual. If the risk does not seem reasonable, it can not with honesty be taken.

Not infrequently a man who has been placed by the State as its representative in charge of an educational unit is confronted by an individual who says, "As a taxpayer, I demand thus and so for my child." Unsupported by any philosophy of public education, the school authority can argue only by meeting the challenge with the same weapons that are threatened. Of course the criterion to be used on such a demand is that evolving from our thesis. If what the taxpayer wants contains a reasonable promise of a dividend to the supporting State, it should be done, not as a concession but as a matter of policy; if it does not, the demand should be shown to be what it really is, a raid on the public treasury for a fancied private profit. In any other department of public works the true issue would be much more readily seen.

So much has been made of the individual and his rights that it is high time for emphasis to be given to the rights of collections of individuals. "Both words, individual and social," writes John Dewey, * "are hopelessly ambiguous, and the ambiguity will never cease so long as we think in terms of an antithesis. The human being whom we fasten upon as individual *par excellence* is moved and regulated by his associations with others; what he does and what the consequences of his behavior are, what his experience consists of, can not even be described, much less accounted for, in isolation." In only a mistaken and short-sighted view can any individual be said to have rights that are opposed to the interests of one or more of the groups with which he is associated. In no instance can his rights transcend those collective rights of the individuals that compose his group; otherwise the rights or interests of the many yield to those of the one. A social philosophy centers attention on the welfare of the group, in which each individual may find opportunities for such development as will contribute his best for their betterment. A restricted view may see conflict, but in reality it simply does not exist.

* The Public and Its Problems, page 186.

There may be, and indeed there often is, conflict, however, because each individual is a member of several groups — his family, his gang, his class, his school, his community, and his State, for instances. Ideally each is or should be related to the larger and enveloping group as an individual is to it. And in no case would a long vision reveal conflict; but actually such idealism does not always prevail: gang may weaken class, and a selfish class intent upon immediate and selfish pleasure may undermine the structure of the school as a whole. It is only natural that an immature youth should magnify the importance of his immediate desires or that he should feel a greater loyalty to those members of the smaller groups with whom he is in continual and intimate contact; but it is a function, and an important function, of education to reveal to him the superior claims and the greater importance of the larger and more remote groups with which he as well as each of the smaller groups likewise is identified. With divided and seemingly conflicting loyalties he lacks the integration that makes for real character and for effective citizenship. If the number who fail of this appreciation is large and the conflicts are important, the integrity of the State is materially weakened. That this distressing result actually exists one can hardly deny, and it exists for the precise reason that education, not being generally and practically conceived as an investment for the perpetuation and betterment of the State, has failed to attempt seriously and with the skills of which it is capable, to seek an integration through showing the obligations to the supporting social group. The emphasis has been too much on privileges, which have come to be conceived as "rights," and too little on responsibilities and obligations.

"The notion that intellect," writes the same distinguished philosopher previously quoted, "is a personal endowment or personal attainment is a great conceit of the intellectual class." It is quite a natural conceit, however, and will persist unless intelligently planned education effectually inculcates ideas of service. Such education though seemingly altruistic, is really and ultimately a contribution to personal as well as to social prosperity and happiness. Whatever case can be made for the selfish development of intellect fails utterly when that development is at the expense of the social group. Certainly it can not be successfully maintained that the public at its own sacrifice appropriates money to educate an individual for the development of powers which will be used selfishly to the detriment of the State. From this negative concept it is only a logical step to the positive statement: the appropriation is made that the individual may be developed so as to be better able and better disposed to contribute to the betterment of the supporting State.

Earlier the term State was defined — loosely but adequately for the discussion at that time. The supporting State in our country widely varies in every respect, especially in size and in wealth. In some sections it continues to be almost wholly a local school district, the boundaries of which are transgressed by practically every social, political, economic, and religious activity; but the tendency is everywhere to increase the size until to some extent it coincides with the county or political state. But if appreciation of larger and still larger social groups, with their obligations, opportunities, and advantages, is desirable, there is at least a suggestion that larger and still larger units undertake some of the responsibilities of support. This suggestion is tremendously strengthened when one reflects how modern inventions of communication and transportation have broken all barriers and have tended to an easy transfer of not only ideas but also of peoples from one community to another. A fiery speech is made in Seattle and a bomb is thrown in New York; the mills of Manchester are closed and children go hungry in the cotton fields of the South; an invention is made in St.

Louis and a few months later its advantages are enjoyed in the most remote parts of the country. No important happening fails to be reported within a few hours to the entire nation. Marvelous as all this seems, it is hardly more striking than the migrations of people. The greatest wealth of every metropolis is made up of the manhood attracted from other communities, which, it should be noted, have paid for the education of the youth who have carried their trained minds and skills to enrich the cities. Official census figures show that 22.2 per cent of our entire population are now living in states other than those in which they were born. It is impossible to oppose the conclusion that the great urban centers, enriched by the contributions of other communities, owe something of their wealth in repayment to the weaker units impoverished by emigration of the manhood that they have paid to educate for their own profit.

This migration has another side, too. Not every immigrant is wholly an asset. Just as maleficent ideas are spread, so impotent and even dangerous men and women pass on from community to community, from state to state. In one year, it is reported, more than 200,000 negroes migrated from the South to the city of New York. No suggestion is made that they were or are bad citizens; but certainly they brought fewer assets to Manhattan than they would have done if they had received a sound education. Many investigators have reported astounding figures of migratory movements in various sections of our country, all without legal let or hindrance of any kind. We prevent the landing on our shores of foreigners who because of poverty, inability to support themselves, disease, immorality, or seditious ideas are likely to become public charges or to endanger our government; but there is no means of barring the way to citizens who for similar reasons may become liabilities or worse. Such a condition and such a fact emphasize that every section of our country is not merely in a fraternal but also in a selfish manner vitally interested in the upbringing and the education of youth in every other section. The only way that this concern can be practically manifested is in participating in the common investment of universal education for mutual protection and advancement. The great variations in economic wealth, in the proportion of children to adults, in the sparseness of population, and in attitudes towards education for all youth make it imperative that the units of taxation be greatly enlarged, that the necessary money be taken from wherever the wealth may be and expended equitably where it is needed. Logic and need point to a far larger participation of the national government in the support of schools than has ordinarily been proposed.

This suggestion at once meets vigorous opposition from a number of sources. It is pointed out that the Federal Constitution makes no specific provision for such participation, nor, it may be noted in rebuttal, does it forbid it. A careful reading of the reports on the constitutional convention reveals that Pinckney and others proposed an article on education, but it was held unnecessary, the power of appropriation already lying with Congress. There is no legal reason why the Federal Government should not meet the new conditions and needs by vastly enlarging its concern with education and increasing the aid that it already gives. The objection that finds its slogan in "States' rights" is merely ignoring the changes that have come with modern civilization. "Paternalism" is a slogan of excuse. Advocates of a protective tariff have shaky ground on which to stand when opposing Federal protection of children, as also have all of us who profit by its activities concerning health, agriculture, commerce, and various other elements of our civilization. If it is paternalism for the Federal Government to collect taxes from the prosperous and expend them equitably for the good of all, wherever they may be, it is similarly paternalism for the state, the county, or the local school district to do so. The beneficent and approved act of the smaller unit would be made merely a more beneficent justice by the larger.

It is freely admitted that what the Federal Government has done in the field of education is open to numerous criticisms, some of them shockingly severe. But failures of the Government — as, for instance, in providing food for our soldiers in Cuba, in leasing public lands, in caring for the Indians — do not argue that it go out of the business concerned. Its failures in education, which are far more of omission than of commission, are due largely to the fact that it has never seriously undertaken responsibility, that it has never conceived education as a long-term investment to return dividends in citizens made better able and better disposed to contribute to the betterment of society.

Opposition to placing the center of gravity in the State rather than in the individual is chiefly the result, when the matter has been seriously considered, of a fear that organized society will ruthlessly and foolishly ignore natural aptitudes, interests, and capacities, designating each child regardless of these characteristics to some activity for which he may not be fitted. Such a fear betrays a gross lack of confidence in the edu-

cational expert and also both in the voice of the
people and in the effectiveness of democratic control. Many of those placed in charge of schools
are inefficient and are likely to make serious mistakes; at present their mistakes are tolerated for
the simple reason that so much secondary education, for which public moneys are expended, is of
no practical importance for either good or evil.
When education is taken as seriously as manufacturing or banking, sufficiently adequate experts will be demanded and produced. No others will be, or should now be, tolerated. The
doctrine of education as an investment by the
State that it may perpetuate itself and promote
its own interests, carries with it far more concern for the individual, for all pupils as individuals, than is shown now for the few who are fortunate enough to have special advocates. The
State can profit only as it recognizes whatever
is unique, whatever is distinctive, in each boy
and girl and develops that as far as it promises
to be profitable to do so.

III

The idea that society should use education
as an instrument for its own good has been far
more potent in several European countries than
it ever has been in the United States. Germany

and France in the nineteenth century, and Russia and Italy at the present time, illustrate nations that carefully planned programs for the perpetuation of the State and for the promotion of its interests by means of education. Dean James Earl Russell has dramatically told the story of Prussia.*

"Just a hundred years ago there was no Germany. Germanic peoples living between the Elbe and the Rhine, grouped in little principalities, each suspicious of the other, were vassals of Napoleon. Their country had been the battlefield of Europe so long that it was a miracle to find any latent spark of nationalism or patriotism. When the night was darkest a system of education was projected, with the University of Berlin in the forefront, a system of education designed from the beginning to make Prussians masters of Germany and, if need be, masters of the world. I need not recount how speedily Prussia threw off the foreign yoke and how gradually she attained her purpose as the dominant power in a United Germany. France, humbled and despoiled, very properly gave the credit of Prussian success, not to German statesmen or military leaders, but to the German schoolmaster. If the schoolmaster in two gen-

* Education for Citizenship, Teachers College Record, March, 1916.

erations could change the home-loving, good-
natured, individualistic German who had been
fought and fought over for centuries by every
war-lord of Europe into the fighting machine
that France found in 1870, and that the rest of
Europe fears to-day; if the schoolmaster could
develop loyalty to a cause, obedience to authority,
cultivate the arts and sciences, develop industry
and direct trade and commerce, it is time that
we learned how it was done. We want to know,
not to imitate the methods or to attain the results,
but chiefly to gain a confidence in our ability to
use other methods in order that we may attain
results worthy of American ideals."

Illustrations of how the program was developed are found in Thomas Alexander's Prussian Elementary Schools,* which was based on
stenographic reports of lessons heard in more
than six hundred classes and which was written
before the World War had come to warp ob-
servations and to distort judgments. In the
pages of this book one finds detailed reports of
instruction through history, literature, music,
and practically every other subject that led to
love of country, devotion to its Kultur, hatred of
its national enemy, and loyalty to the ruling family. It is with reluctance that the limits of space
are recognized and copious quotations are

* The Macmillan Company.

omitted. The general story is well summarized in the following paragraphs by Reisner:*

"The German boy and girl have been educated in an emotional atmosphere of patriotism. The instruction in German has been designed to fill them with pride in their native tongue and make them conversant with its masterpieces, particularly those which strengthened the spirit of devotion to the fatherland. The German patriotic poems, sometimes set to thrilling music, have woven their spell over youthful minds for more than a century, and every effort has been made, through the selection of suitable materials and the emphasis placed upon learning them by heart, to build up in the boys and girls an emotional set that would cause them unhesitatingly to give themselves without reservation at their country's need. Those old poems, with their glorification of national virtues, their recalling of ancient hatreds, their passionate praise of courage and self-sacrifices in the national cause, have done much to mould the German people into national unity.

"The German schools, and particularly the lower schools, have exhibited in a preëminent degree the pragmatic as opposed to the scientific

* Reisner, Edward H., Nationalism and Education since 1789. By permission of The Macmillan Company, publishers.

conception of the teaching of history. The German schools have taught history not so much to develop the power of making sound judgments in regard to social problems as to establish a certain emotional bias that might even resist the admission of new data capable of modifying that bias. In this type of history-teaching the Prussian teacher has enjoyed an advantageous position, for Prussia, down to the year 1918, had experienced only one successful political tradition. The rise to territorial, military, and economic greatness of Prussia and Germany has taken place under the Hohenzollern dynasty and under social institutions which have been the least modified in the direction of liberal democracy of any of the Great Powers of Western Europe. . . . Prussian history has been such that the teacher did not need to be critical. He might explain away difficulties, such as the partitions of Poland and the seizure of Alsace-Lorraine, on the basis of military necessity or of missionary zeal. He might paint up the occasional nonentities of the Hohenzollern line, whitewash the eccentrics and the debauchees, and laud the characteristics and achievements of the really great. . . . We know from our own national experience that it is easy to accept a complimentary bias toward one's own country, and can well understand the same fact as respects

Germany. The German teacher of history could exhibit France as a rapacious conqueror in taking Alsace and Lorraine, with their predominantly German population, and use that fact as justification for the taking back on Germany's part of the 'lost provinces.' In the same way he could minimize the taking of so large a share of the territory of the assassinated nationality of Poland on the ground that if Prussia had not taken it Russia would have done so to the great danger of Prussian interests. How easily, too, the social and political ameliorations which have taken place since the Treaty of Tilsit might be attributed to the benevolence of the ruling house. Through following such methods, the teacher of history in the Prussian primary school has been a preacher of patriotism and the official apologist of the reigning dynasty and of the established social and political order.

"The teaching of geography has also ministered to national unity. The question, 'What is Germany?' is reported to have been asked in a German school, and the answer prompted by the teacher was, 'Germany is a land entirely surrounded by enemies.' The incident in its details may be true or not, but it certainly illustrates aptly enough the use which that subject has been put to in the German schools. The nationalistic influence of geography begins with the emphasis which is placed on national and local geography, tied up as it is with the study of history. The pupil thus comes to love not only the national heroes but the very ground on which they walked. We in America have difficulty in appreciating this factor, for our cities and towns are all so new. They have little of stirring history and tradition connected with them. The case is different in Germany, where almost every city and countryside have been the scene of some striking historical episode.

"The German boy and girl were not left ignorant of the great geographical factors which conditioned national life. The difficulty of defending eastern Prussia against Russian attack was no less known to the children on the benches of the primary schools than it was to the Imperial War College at Berlin. The menace to Germany, under the necessity of importing food and raw materials from overseas, of the undisputed naval power of Great Britain, became an argument in the child's mind for naval expansion and the acquisition of a colonial empire. The teaching of geography was carried out, in part at least, with the intention of making the child intelligent about national economic and military problems and convinced of the necessity and the justice of national policies." These facts can be abundantly supplemented.

It must be noted and emphasized that the Prussian program of education, which until the outbreak of hostilities in 1914 probably had no superior for careful planning and for effectiveness, was formulated by Fichte and a small body of fellow philosophers in the early years of the nineteenth century. These men were able to make their remarkable contribution to national progress primarily because they clearly realized, as our several governments have done in only a vague and indefinite way, the power of education and the necessity of the State's using it to perpetuate itself and to promote its own interests. Furthermore they had the courage of their convictions, and so laid down the broad principles of a program that was consistently developed in the subsequent decades by all the power and devotion of educational leaders carefully trained for their responsibilities and obligations. The formulation of such a program leading toward the ideals of our government would be a monumental mark of progress. Its lack not only evidences our failure to conceive education seriously but it also constitutes a fundamental weakness and a constant threat to democratic society. Such efforts as have been made have resulted from the labors of individuals or small groups, working without the sanction of any adequately authoritative body — and in some instances contrary to what could have been approved by a more representative agency.

When we turn to France of the nineteenth century, and in a less definite way at the present time, we find a similar use of education, especially on the secondary school level, for perpetuating the State and for promoting its interests. The program in the lycées and collèges though definite to the Latin intelligence is difficult to explain concisely to an American, but it exists nevertheless and commands as few other matters can do the devoted concern of national leaders. In the midst of the pressing problems of reparation and of financial stabilization, the Chamber of Deputies devoted an entire month a few years ago to discussing proposed changes in the secondary school curriculum. Reisner * presents an exposition of the contribution of the elementary schools, from which the following paragraphs may be quoted:

"No less prominent in this instruction than the desire to promote patriotism is the purpose of making the child feel the superior excellence of the political institutions of the Third Republic. Many of the manuals contain liberal extracts from the 'Declaration of the Rights of Man' or reproduce it in full, for this statement

* Opus cit., pages 86 ff.

— which was a part of the Constitution of 1791 — has since then been associated in France with political liberalism. The official program of studies also makes it a special exercise to explain the meaning of the Republican motto, 'Liberty, Equality, and Fraternity.' The manuals give many indications of the purpose of the present government to perpetuate its existence through the inculcation of Republican principles upon the youth. To this end, the disadvantages of the *ancien régime* of privilege and autocracy are used as foils for the description of the enlarged personal opportunity and security under the present system of political organization."

"The competition which the Third Republic has had to meet has not been limited to the menace of a possible return to monarchy, but it has included as well the perhaps more real menace of Socialism. Against the Socialist political theories the school instruction in morals and civics has carried on as definite a campaign as against the monarchical principle. The Third Republic has undertaken to tutor the youth of France not only in regard to what they should believe concerning kings, but also in regard to what might ensue upon laboring-class control and a radical disturbance of the existing financial and industrial organization of society."

Soviet Russia is too new for its program to be

developed in all of its details, but that it has recognized the power of education for its maintenance and development, indeed for the very preservation of its government, is patent from all reports, both sympathetic and hostile, that have come out of the country. Aversion to the ideals and the principles of the Soviets should not blind us to the wisdom that they have shown in recognizing the power of education to inculcate the knowledge, the attitudes, and the loyalties necessary to perpetuate and to promote the form of society that has been established. The devotion and diligence that are being manifest to develop an education likely to pay such dividends as they want may well put us to shame and stimulate us to similar activity for the maintenance and the betterment of the ideals which we have accepted and approved as superior.

According to Rul, a liberal Russian newspaper published in Berlin, the Soviet government has decided to examine all university professors to insure that only those who are sympathetic with the new ideals have the privilege of influencing youth. "If some eminent scientists are displaced, the proletariat," says the Krassnaya Gazette, "will soon produce others of equally high merit." Preference in secondary and higher education is reported as given to sons and daughters of workingmen. The curriculum has been violently revised to insure that all subject matter, "coördinating with the theory of Marxism and Leninism," shall contribute to the desired ends. Old methods of instruction are being rapidly replaced by modern and more useful ones, the influence of Daltonism and of John Dewey being marked. And George Seldes has reported * extraordinary efforts to extend education to soldiers and other adults, all for one end, the strengthening of the society that furnishes the schooling.

Italy, too, under the *régime* of Mussolini, has learned the power of education to do more than impart academic skills and the heritage of the past. Recently the secretary of the Fascist party said: "The liberal university, where existed the greatest coquetry of intellectual liberty, socialism, and philosophy; where one could teach anti-clericalism, anti-colonialism, renunciation, anti-militarism, and the like; the university where one admired more freely the professor opposing the state than the orthodox professor; in which the 'right of laziness' of the students corresponded to the right of every single professor of exhibiting his own ethics, his own irreligion, his own politics — certainly this university ought to die." Accompanying this statement was an

* Seldes, George, You Can't Print That. Payson and Clarke. 1929.

order that "no professor may teach in the higher schools of Italy unless he is approved by the Fascist party," which is the government, "and given a tessera, a little booklet on the order of a passport. And this tessera is not given unless the instructor declares himself in full accord with the principles of Mussolini's government." More than this, the teachers are required to be active in the Fascisti and propagandists for their doctrines.

These facts are illustrations of what is being done on all levels of education. "Recent orders of educational authorities are to the effect that school directors shall arrange to have each teacher add this instruction to the school program, and that it is to be adapted to the intellectual capacities of the different school groups and introduced naturally as part of the new culture. The field to be covered includes: The corporate State; the syndicates; the Great Council; Dopolavoro, an organization for the wise use of leisure time; Balilla, a national boys' and girls' organization; the organization for motherhood and childhood; the general progress of the country; and the principal works of local, regional, and national interest. The Labor Charter, in particular, is to be read and its principles expounded."

This brief exposition of how foreign governments with ideals and objectives radically different from our own have used education for the preservation and promotion of what they esteem essential for the good of their respective States is a dangerous adventure in polemics. At least, it would be dangerous if it were addressed to popular rather than to intelligent readers, for those in whom education has not developed a supremacy of the calm intellect over prejudices and passions might illogically conclude that the argument is for us to follow identical patterns. This is not the point at all. An endeavor has been made to show that other States — in these instances, European national governments — have been wise enough to recognize that by means of education and by means of education chiefly each could insure the maintenance of its ideals and their direction. Each has had a different set of mediate objectives and each has, in consequence, used a different curriculum for insuring dividends on its investment.

It would be a great mistake, a suicidal mistake, for us to adopt or to imitate the objectives or the exact methods of foreign governments. It would be a similar mistake for us not to recognize the need and the wisdom of planning and of working for the perpetuation of all that we consider good in our societal organizations and for the constant direction of their development upward. The illustrations have shown that foreign governments have found education to be an efficacious and a necessary means to their ends. That their ends are offensive should not blind us, as it does those who think with their prejudices, to the wisdom of planning a program of education that will assuredly pay dividends on our great investment to make the State a better place in which to live and in which to make a living. It is only foolish and short-sighted pride that leads any one to a confidence in national supremacy because of natural resources or of innate powers of a people. If education is used by other states for the development of attitudes and ideals hostile to those to which we are committed, then education must be used by us even more skilfully to insure superior results in the inevitable and eternal conflicts of philosophies of life. That certain nations have prostituted their schools to achieve special privileges for the ruling classes is no reason why we should not intelligently and skilfully use them for the general good. Their results for selfishness reveal what we may achieve for altruism. Once we as a people have recognized the power of education and the principle of public support for public good, we have before us only the tedious but entirely possible program of developing plans that will justify the experiment of universal education on which we have embarked and of assuring satisfactory dividends on the great investment.

Other and usually non-social groups have more quickly and more practically than the State recognized the power of education to influence maturing youth for definite desired ends. Reference here is not made to the activities of socially minded groups or individuals who from time to time have brought pressure upon the schools and who have generously contributed aid to introduce and to promote neglected subjects, such as music, health, safety, home economics, the vocations, and extra-curricula interests, or such auxiliary agencies as the visiting teacher, lunch rooms, clinics, and libraries. What we have in mind is the propaganda of organized groups who wish to use the schools for the promotion of their own purposes, which usually, but not always, seen in isolation, are good. Every administrator can give evidence of the pressure, often irresistible, that is brought to bear on the schools to turn aside from their prepared programs and give instruction, in "weeks" or "days" or "drives," on the constitution, home products, public utilities, thrift, the stock exchange, and the glorification of mother, dad, apples, prunes, the goldenrod, or yeast. These subjects vary from those "to which we could give substantial and hearty approval, through matters not of any great importance to the public, to things which have a purely selfish motive associated with them."

Care is required to discriminate, at one extreme, between the perfectly proper and laudable effort of active groups to influence school programs, against the lethargy of traditionally minded teachers, toward the introduction of units of teaching that should meet neglected needs, and, at the other, the propaganda to prostitute the schools for selfish ends. Recently we have had offered to the schools lessons on public utilities prepared and proffered with the bait of no cost by the corporations which own the franchises and which presumably would profit by the impartation of the data presented. The New York Stock Exchange employs a skilled and charming agent who speaks without charge to high school assemblies, explaining the organization and activities of the Exchange, presumably to break down the public hostility that long existed. A great newspaper promotes a nationwide oratorical contest on the constitution, using such skill in developing its program that administrators feel themselves forced to devote more time in their schools to this one topic than many of them consider wise. Societies offer to the schools their returned missionaries to tell of conditions and "the need" in foreign lands; other schools send out jubilee singers; and Rotary Clubs are always willing to furnish a speaker to "boost" some project that they have initiated.

Now, as already stated, all of these activities are not bad. The illustrations, chosen from among many possible ones, are presented primarily to support the point that outside agencies have recognized and are vigorously attempting to use the power of the schools to influence youth toward ideas, ideals, attitudes, and prejudices which, they hope and expect, will ultimately lead to actions favorable to the promoting cause. Acceptance of the thesis defended in this essay makes inevitable two questions concerning such proposals by outside agencies to influence the work of the schools: first, does each one promise an increase of dividends in good citizenship? And, second, what is its relative value in the program as a whole? If the answers, as returned by those experts most competent to make them, are favorable to any proposal, it should be definitely incorporated into the curriculum and given such emphasis as its importance warrants. It should be accepted and used because it promises a material contribution to social good and not because some individual or some organization, however locally strong, brings pressure to bear for its occasional adoption, which inevitably disturbs the prepared program. One reason, of course, why such extraneous proposals meet a hospitable reception is that they often promise more obvious good than what they would replace. This fact brings no credit to the inertia that retards curriculum reconstruction consistent with modern needs; rather it is a revelation of shameful neglect on the part of social democracy to use the schools as intelligently as it might to perpetuate itself and to promote its highest interests.

Not infrequently we find propaganda supported by legislation, which has been procured by interested and active groups. Legislation in behalf of some project considered good in itself without any one's taking the trouble to relate it to fundamental principles or to the program as a whole, seems fairly easy to procure. The legislative bodies of our several states, without having or even professing expertness in education or social philosophy, have placed on the statute books numerous requirements concerning what the schools shall teach. When these are genuine expressions of the social will, approved by expert representatives of the people, well and good; but they are far from always being that. "Some one is always trying to grab the schools for the sake of grabbing society." Active minorities become dominant through the failure of the teaching profession to have a philosophy clear and comprehensive enough to construct a program so convincing to the public that it can not recklessly be tampered with by laymen. When it has that, it will be granted by the public more respect and authority than it now has.

The public has by long experience become increasingly sensitive to political interference with the schools. The election and retention of administrators and teachers influenced by partisan politics, the expenditure of public moneys favoring political henchmen, and the locating of schools on sites approved by those politically influential have happily become so infrequent that their reported occurrence causes a scandal. But political interference with what the schools teach, if it has the appearance of plausibility, is too common and too complacently accepted, even if it has no sound support in educational philosophy and in facts expertly determined. This situation will continue until education is conceived as a public investment carefully made that society may be bettered, until the curriculum proves its importance by obviously and materially affecting the lives of those that follow it. The education of most importance is dangerous: it influences youth concerning how it shall feel toward important social, political, and economic matters, and consequently how it shall act. The public has never been greatly concerned with what is taught in the abstract academic subjects, for the simple reason that their effects are too intangible and remote, if they exist at all, to manifest any change in what are considered the important matters of living. But it has and does manifest concern regarding those subjects which definitely and immediately make boys and girls act differently. It may almost be said that education that is not dangerous is not important. Perhaps the general sense of the public in this matter has a direct suggestion to educators complacent in the routine of innocuous tradition.

Yielding to interested and active minority groups, however they may be actuated, in the matter of curriculum modification is not evidence of a recognition of the need of social dividends or of the tremendous power of the schools to pay them. "The pathways of democracy," as Suzzallo has brilliantly said, "are not to be chosen by any one class or group," not even by devoted and conscientious teachers. "The teacher works under social limitations," and should have direction of the best experts with a broad social view and an understanding of the reasons for education supported at public expense. "Educational freedom," Suzzallo continues, "is not identical with individual freedom.

When the teacher teaches, he represents organized society and civilization, and not merely himself. Once he enters the classroom he stands for both more and less than himself. He must not confuse his private views with his public duties. . . . The schools should no more be subject to the private partisanship of a teacher than to the organized propaganda of groups outside the school. Long ago it was settled that we should not impose our private religion and our partisan politics on our pupils. Similarly we have no right now, directly or indirectly, to insinuate into the plastic minds of youth our private doctrines or conclusions on current and unsettled economic and social issues."

What is the wisdom of freeing the schools from politics, of generously supporting them, and of "giving every child his chance" unless concern is manifested that the highest good of the supporting State is sought? The propagandist for private gain and even the individual devoted to his private program which has not gained social sanction may inject a toxin that has far-reaching and deleterious effects if he is not opposed by an enlightened and quickened public sentiment. It is only human for any person to use, if he can, the powerful agency of the schools to achieve ends that he considers good for himself or in his limited view good for his group. Unless his project is not only good, but also the highest good possible under the circumstances, for the social group that supports the schools for its own benefit, his activities smack strongly of treason — unconscious and unintended perhaps, but treason none the less, for it undermines or weakens the program that has been set up for the larger good. It is only common sense and common prudence that the State, conceiving education seriously as a means of maintaining itself on ever higher levels, should take all necessary steps to insure a curriculum program that promises the largest dividends of the kind desired and should constantly and vigorously protect it from interference by inexpert meddlers.

One can not follow far along the line of thinking set up by the thesis that education is a public investment for the perpetuation of the State and the promotion of its interests without coming upon the problem of private schools in a democracy. This is a dangerous topic, but that is no reason why we should not examine it somewhat and consider the conclusions which are indicated. The State — that is, as before defined, organized society — is concerned that it be maintained and that it be bettered for the good of all the individuals composing it. In order to preserve itself and to make possible the richest, happiest lives consistent with the ideals that constitute the bases of its structure, it restrains by its mores and by force the minority that would violate its canons; it refuses to admit immigrants who hold materially different philosophies of life and government; and it provides an education presumably to promote in the young a loyalty to approved ideals and to inculcate knowledge and skills that lead toward their attainment. To insure that such an education as is essential in a democracy is obtained, the State not only provides the schools free of all cost but also compels attendance until childhood ceases, and in numerous ways encourages further attendance during youth and young adulthood.

Along with this program, which so far as stated seems eminently sensible and long-sighted, the State, as represented in its several political units, permits private schools to be conducted under various auspices, approves attendance on them as satisfying all requirements of education, and ordinarily gives them no supervision at all or, at best, one that is merely perfunctory. This policy may not be equally sensible and long-sighted. · It is true that the majority of private schools follow the general academic program of the public schools, but in many, perhaps most, cases they are not required to do so. Moreover, with a few exceptions of slight significance, they can teach whatever philosophies of life they please. This remarkable privilege is even subsidized, for those schools not conducted for profit, by the remission of taxes. American born children may freely be taught doctrines devotion to which would exclude the alien from landing on our shores. They may be taught history which ridicules national heroes and places on a pedestal those who have carried the flag of hostile philosophies, economics which in our judgment undermines our entire economic structure, literature which inculcates ideals subversive to those that guide our conduct, and music which promotes loyalty to alien lands and rulers. In few instances, of course, do they teach in any of these ways; but the fact that they may do so is remarkable evidence not so much of considered freedom as of failure to realize the potency of education for vitally affecting conduct that materially contributes to the building up or to the weakening of the State.

If any private schools teach doctrines subversive to the interest of the State or omit the teaching of those that are considered important, and even essential, to its welfare, the fact betrays a significant weakness in our policy. There is reason to believe that the freedom allowed is in no inconsiderable number of cases abused. If this point were developed and illustrated, attention would doubtless be directed away from the main thesis, on which it is desired that it be focused. The teaching of such doctrines as are hostile to those generally approved by a democratic society fails to receive the rebuke and the prohibition that it deserves primarily because we have not so realized the importance of education in perpetuating and promoting the State as to provide an effective program looking in this direction. No substantial objection can be made to private schools until the State has determined an educational program that is of obvious and convincing value to general social interests.

During the past few years masters of private institutions of instruction have affected the term "independent schools." This precisely emphasizes the chief objection to them: they are independent of control or regulation by the State. No institution that influences or declares its intention of influencing the youth who will soon be citizens can the State afford to permit to be wholly independent. For its own safety and the insurance of its perpetuation and promotion it must approve their programs, inspect their work, and measure their results, not merely academic achievement but also the whole complex of attitudes and ideals that affect the students as members of society.

Not only may independent schools to a large extent teach what they please and neglect to teach what the expert representatives of society have found, or should find, to be essential in our society, but they have other effects that are similarly bad. They tend to weaken or to destroy the interest of their patrons in public education. It is unusual to find a man who sends his children to a private school at the same time active in the promotion of public education and generous in his support of it. Exceptions do exist, and as exceptions they are conspicuous. The generous and occasionally princely donations of patrons to the upbuilding of private schools would have been beneficent contributions to society if turned to the improvement of popular education. Sometimes they excuse the withheld greater by proffering the lesser. It is often stated that the private schools, benefiting by munificence of patrons, are free to experiment and thus to lead public schools to superior practices. Whatever is possible, the fact remains that a relatively small number, almost an insignificant number, of private schools have in the past engaged in any pioneering important to public schools or are doing so to-day. The exceptions can be matched fifty for one by those that are reactionary and complacent. It is a safe statement that to-day the experimenting most significant

for social welfare is being done in schools under
public control. It is in them that the new and
reasonable philosophy of education and the findings of scientific researches have found most
fertile soil. And if education is an essential instrument of democracy, the experimentation
ought to be done with public funds under democratic conditions. The set ups in the notable
private experimental schools are too artificial
to make easy transfer of their findings to public
schools.

It is often argued that the private school is
justified because it makes special provision for
the exceptional child, the one who for one reason or another does not fit into the program for
mass education. If the State does not provide
for such a child, though indeed it often does,
the chief reason is that the adults immediately
concerned are content to give a certain exceptional child special privileges and feel small sense
of responsibility for civic activity that would result in similar provisions for all with similar
needs. A truly democratic State plays no fa-
vorites. It is equally concerned with all of its
children that they may be made better able and
better disposed to contribute maximally to the
betterment of society. What is good for one exceptional child should be made possible for all
that have similar needs. The chief difference in

this matter between the parent and the parental State is that the former exerts himself to give his children special privileges insuring an advantageous start in life; the latter is committed to giving all its children such advantages as will insure an equal start.

The very segregation of children in private schools with the pretension of affording special privileges, whether they do or not, makes it difficult for them not to look on themselves as in one sense or another superior to the masses, who have to attend public schools. "Nothing," writes Dean Inge in Labels and Libels, "has contributed so much to create 'two nations' in England as the tradition of a 'gentleman's education.'" Many parents who have sought for their children special advantages are regretfully conscious of a loss in them of democratic sentiments. They may have gained many other things, but in greater or in less degree they have lost or have never acquired a faith in democracy and a genuine understanding and of sympathy for the common man. These are gained by association that breeds respect rather than by abstract instruction in isolation.

There is such a variety of private schools that it is difficult to think of them all subsumed under one name. There are those conducted merely for the personal profit of proprietors, those to

provide special privileges for pupils who can
otherwise not be fittingly cared for, those orig-
inally instituted for social good and still linger-
ing in a land where the function is usually better
served by the public institutions, those that are
active in experimentation and in pioneering new
paths through the wilderness, a group that could
contribute quite as much or more if devoting
their resources to the pressing problems of democratic education under normal conditions, and
those supported by religious, "benevolent," or
political organizations to promote their doctrines. Consider them all, the entire 2500 of
them on a secondary level, and ask if they contribute enough either to the ends for which they
are supported or, what is more important, to
democratic society to justify their existence.
Whatever criticism is leveled at the public
schools, they are by and large more abundantly
justified than the private schools. Even most
of those under religious auspices would be found
educationally bankrupt with any competent
audit. With the chief exception of one class,
they seek their ends by a perfunctory reading of
the Scriptures, which has apparently little precip-
itate in moral conduct, by a compulsory religious
"chapel" or assembly, which is usually so re-
sented by students as to negative the intended
good effects, by Bible courses, which even if they

reach the majority of the student body have yet
to prove their beneficence, and sometimes by an
annual "revival," which is significant in its con-
trast to the activities of the rest of the year. The
boasted "atmosphere" and the "personal influence" are not peculiar to private schools. Both
exist wherever good men and women have been
selected as teachers and directed by an intelligent
administrator alert to his responsibility.

Ask further the extent to which private schools
are, on the whole, a handicap rather than an as-
sistance to the program of perpetuating and promoting the interests of a common society. It is
exceedingly doubtful if unprejudiced findings
would substantiate the independent school on
the basis either of theory or of accomplishment.
The few that are conspicuously successful for
both individual and public good shield a multi-
tude that are successful for only the first or for
neither. In all probability, lacking as we do
such a pragmatic philosophy as has been repeatedly advocated, independent schools will continue, though their number and importance have
relatively dwindled; but in theory they have as a
class small justification. In practice they can
not and do not contribute as the public school
can be made to do to the perpetuation and promotion of the democratic State. When society
conceives education with the importance that its

possibilities justify and when it has prepared a program consistent with its need, the private school will no longer be required or tolerated.

IV

When first presented, the thesis that education is a long-term investment by the State to make itself a better place in which to live and in which to make a living, to perpetuate itself and to promote its own interests, may have seemed not only reasonable but also innocuous. Undoubtedly some of the conclusions drawn have seemed so radical as to be offensive, so contrary to what is generally accepted as to arouse resentments that make difficult dispassionate consideration of the argument. As a rule it is emotionally disturbing to have conventional "opinions" attacked, whether or not they have been arrived at by intelligent processes. It is hoped that education has been so effective that each reader will calmly and thoroughly consider every application on its merits, constantly referring to the fundamental thesis. If any application is unwarranted, to what does the accepted principle lead? If the basic principle is rejected, what is the justification for the expenditure of public funds for universal and free education? And to what conclusions does the substituted principle lead?

Surely any reflective thinker will realize that our present policy is so lacking in a philosophic basis that is generally understood, by professional educators as well as by laymen, as to endanger the continued support of public schools and to give unsatisfactory direction for their further development.

By no means all of the implications of the proposed thesis have been presented. If the principle of public support for education has been sufficiently brought into the focus of attention, with illustrations enough of its importance to give it emphasis, we may well trust the intelligence of the profession and of laymen alike to make application to all the problems that are involved. "The indirect and unthought of consequences," as Dewey has said in another connection, "are usually more important than those that immediately appear." To stimulate thought on the matter a few of the further implications are now stated, with brief comment on each.

If education is supported as an investment it should be required to pay dividends. This principle should govern the formulation of general and specific objectives, the preparation of the curriculum, the selection and retention of personnel, the choice of methods, the types of organization, the retention and guidance of students — in short, the entire educational program. To it would be subordinated all matters of pedagogy, which in it would find meaning and direction.

The desired dividends should be definitely determined. What is the good State? What makes it a better place in which to live? What makes it a better place in which to make a living? What are characteristics of the good life? Answers to such questions can not, and should not, be made with finality, but until after serious search they are tentatively postulated with considerable definiteness, it is futile to expect education to be more than traditional, decorative, or fortuitously successful. Appreciation of the necessity of dividends on the great investment of education may lead society to make serious effort to formulate acceptably definite answers. Such a demand would bring philosophers out of their alcoves and prove their worth to society. A coöperative endeavor to realize the objectives of education would give direction to life itself. Until definitions of the good life and the good State are more generally understood, education must fall short of the important contributions of which it is capable.

Based upon such tentative definitions a new curriculum must be formulated, a new curriculum that consistently looks toward the betterment of society through the betterment of the

individual.   Lacking certainty as to the exact
nature of all goods — or, rather, as to the relative
values of the goods that are generally recognized
— we may well be generous in our inclusions
and charitable to all proposals, whether they be
found in tradition or in the radical new phenomena of life; but there is urgent need, both
to remedy wastes of money, time, and effort
and to insure dividends, that such a program
of studies be formulated.   Flexner well says that
"nothing should be unproved."   The initial criterion for testing the values of elements in the new
curriculum must be the probability of contributions to social needs.   During the past few years
a wave of enthusiasm has surged and resurged
across our country for curriculum revision.
Convinced of the need, especially in secondary
schools, the public has approved and appropriated
funds — in some cases with apparent generosity,
but never sufficient for the importance of the
proposed undertaking — and committees have
set to work with varying degrees of enthusiasm.
The results, even the best of them, have been
pathetically small and tragically unsatisfactory.
Why?   Partly because the task is too tremendous to be accomplished with the utterly inadequate machinery that has been provided —
usually teachers contributing in the interstices of
their regular duties, — but chiefly because there

has been no adequate conception that the primary step is the formulation of a clear, comprehensive, and pragmatic philosophy, the initial item of which concerns the desiderata of the good life in a democratic State. Only with this as a beginning a list of assured and probable values in the curriculum can be sought with any probability of significant success.

The new curriculum, based on a recognition of the need to pay dividends in social good on the great public investment, will not neglect what is traditionally academic, but it will be far more comprehensive than any curriculum of ours has ever been in the past. It will need to be, for life is far more complex and extensive, for individuals on every level of culture, than it has ever been before. The new curriculum will seek social integration, the unifying for happy and effective living of all members of the various groups by knowledge, ideals, and practices. It will be concerned with attitudes, each one infused by an approving emotion, quite as truly as with information; and it will always aim at action in conduct. It will make curricular such of the present extra-curricula activities as can prove their worth. It will be guided primarily by the obligation to pay satisfactory dividends to the supporting State, and being thus guided it will be a new curriculum indeed, for by the wildest stretch of the imagination what is now taught in the conventional high schools pays such inadequate dividends that the State, if it depended on them alone for its wealth, would long ago have been hopelessly bankrupt.

The new curriculum will be appropriate to all students. As in any profitable industry, the school will seek to work up all its raw material so that each type will attain its highest value. There will be no dump heap of ejected failures. After the preliminary processes, the education essential to all in a democracy at whatever cost of time and money, there will be increasing differentiation according to needs and capacities, and every type of education that promises dividends on the social investment will for that reason be respectable and respected. Abstract academic education will be respectable for those whose abilities can assimilate it for social good, however remote; and concrete vocational education will be respectable for others differently gifted.

This ideal, which is generally accepted in theory by trained educators, has too little application in practice. Seventy per cent of our secondary schools are too small to permit under present practices of any satisfactory degree of differentiation; in the remainder it is provided far, far less than it could be. We must find a way out. We shall do so only when the desirability is conceived as a necessity, when the waste of the attempted fitting of all to Procrustes' bed is realized as destruction of the vital assets of society. Guidance must be a more important part of the new program, and guidance that is sound and beneficent is possible only when junior high schools satisfactorily perform their functions of exploration of each youth's interests, aptitudes, and capacities and of revealing to him the possibilities in and the requirements of the various advanced fields of all the most important kinds. With this experience the youth is prepared to coöperate with his parents and his teachers in planning a program that promises most to him and most to the society that makes it possible. Such a program will for this reason be respectable and important.

Both exploration and revelation must be by means of materials and experiences that are, so far as possible, of assured values in themselves. Life is too precious, even in childhood and youth, to be gambled away on remotely contingent values. We may well learn a lesson from the industrialist who finds what each part of his raw material is good for, and then works it up according to its promise of dividends. All of the raw material of the schools is valuable for something; and as all of it will inevitably enter into

the social complex, it being possible to throw
none of it upon the dump of inactivity, education
has precisely the challenge of making each youth
maximally good for the highest kind of life he
can be prepared to lead, or else it fails of its responsibility. No dividends are paid when efforts are wastefully and unwisely expended in
attempting to prepare him for what there is no
evidence that he can do with satisfaction to
society.

Secondary education has been handicapped by
the tradition that it is most respectable only
when it is preparing for institutions of higher
learning. So respectable is this tradition that
any critic of it at once places himself in jeopardy
before those who have been stamped with degrees, whether they still contain the administered
cultures or not. In self-defense let me hasten
to say that I believe in higher academic education — for all who can acquire it and profit from
it; I believe that it should be provided by the
State for all who can so master it as to pay dividends of any desirable kinds to society. I go
even farther: I believe in higher education for
every youth, appropriate to his needs and continuing until it ceases to pay dividends commensurate with the cost in money and in time.
But this is a different kind of devotion to higher
education from that which conceives the term to

include only advanced liberal or professional studies. These are highly desirable and highly profitable when sought by those whom they can materially advance toward successful living; they are worse than waste when they are pursued, often at a great distance, by those incompetent in these fields. Merely because collegiate education of the usual kind is "higher," it is not therefore suitable for all youth; it is a profitable investment at any one's cost only when evidence has been adduced that it is likely to pay desirable dividends. Merely because it is traditionally a mark of the leisure class, to which such an increasing number now aspire as to have destroyed much of its significance in this respect, it is not necessarily a good investment for the State to provide it for all. Evidence that it is not the curriculum of higher education that makes it attractive to most students is failure of the majority to pursue advanced courses when they have the opportunity or independently to continue their studies and interests after graduation.

Secondary schools are handicapped, then, because of the expectation that they shall prepare for higher education of academic kinds more students than are fit to profit by it. They handicap themselves by inculcating in their students a conviction that much of their curriculum is of value only as a preparation for further study in the remote future, that "man never is, but always (is) to be blest." Unfortunately the conviction is in far too many cases well founded. The thesis of this essay requires that all courses on the secondary school level be of maximum good to the extent to which they are pursued. Otherwise there is no assurance of desirable dividends on the investment by the State. When there is a consistent attempt to formulate courses good so far forth, the effect will be twofold: first, it will tremendously increase the assured value of the secondary school courses; and, second, it will prepare students of unusual capacity for really profitable pursuit of the courses offered by the colleges. Unless propaedeutic courses are profitable in themselves or, what in our present knowledge is only with severe limitations possible, unless they are restricted to those who will assuredly continue into profitable study on advanced levels, they can not be successfully defended as a part of the program offered at public expense ultimately for public good.

Everywhere in this discussion the making of a living has been subordinated to the making of a rich life. This is as it should be. But if education is to be successful, if it is to pay dividends, it must also prepare men and women comfortably to support themselves and their families. To do this they must somewhere procure training in a vocation. The desirable guidance previously mentioned would also include direction toward the highest type of vocation in which each individual can be successful and happy. Vocational effectiveness of its citizens is essential to the State, and vocational effectiveness of the optimum kind can not be insured unless the State provides in its system of education training for it.

There has been a strange reluctance of the State to commit itself to vocational education. This is due, of course, in part to the strength of the traditional academic curriculum, in part to the lack of agreement and of consistency among the educational specialists in the field, and in part to the complexity, the difficulty, and the cost of any comprehensive program. And yet, whatever the obstacles and difficulties, the thesis that education is a State investment points very clearly at the necessity of dividends from vocational effectiveness. For various reasons the States have been inconsistent and discriminatory in their policy; they have, in some degree at least, helped to an education those who aspired to be ministers, lawyers, doctors, engineers, and teachers, and on lower levels those who were preparing for clerical work. But the greatest number of future citizens have had to discover for themselves vocations, often of a type lower than they were competent for, and to find uneconomical and limited training on the jobs. Such discrimination is not consistent with democracy; and, what is more, it does not promise such dividends from all citizens, effective and happy in their work, as the State needs. It is of course true that some vocations require advanced professional study; some, on the other hand, can be adequately prepared for on the secondary school level; and some may perhaps best be learned on the job. But even for the last kind education can insure more effective learning by preparation and by coöperation. The necessity of dividends to society in men and women skilled and happy in the highest vocations for which they are by nature fitted clearly points to the concern of the State with vocational education.

A negative implication of importance is that nothing is justified in the curriculum that does not promise to pay satisfactory dividends on the great investment of education. The immediate objection made is that one can not foretell what will prove profitable. Within limits this is true, and yet certainly no one would argue that on this account the curriculum should cover all extant knowledge and prepare for every possible contingency, an ideal that transcends all reason. The very richness of our heritage forces a choice of some kind, and in making the choice we should be guided both positively and negatively by the principle of social investment. What promises a reasonable return to the State, directly or indirectly, can be justified in the public school curriculum; what does not, can not be. Seldom in the business world can an investor say with absolute certainty what will pay best; but by using the best judgment that he has he remains solvent and becomes prosperous. He carefully measures the results of what has been tried in the past, he reflects on changes in needs and demands, he considers his raw materials and his operatives, and his equipment, and then he plans as wisely as he can. There is no less obligation on those responsible for the best possible program for expending public funds on education.

Closely related to this is the implication that no student should be permitted to pursue at the State's expense courses which his record shows he is not likely to assimilate with profit to himself and with consequent profit to society. This point has already been sufficiently elaborated. Our present practice is not only to permit, but in cases even to encourage or to compel, the pursuance of courses by individual students whose past record and known characteristics give every indication of failure or of wholly inadequate returns of profit. By the criterion of reasonable social dividends on the investment by the State the school may safely exclude students from courses, even from those which for selfish reasons they or their parents demand. The burden of proof, after all existing evidence has been considered, is on the student. If he manifests previously undemonstrated resources of ability, or industry, or information, the decision may, of course, properly be reconsidered. But the general principle holds that school officers can in honesty to the employing State permit no individual program that does not reasonably promise not only returns but also the maximum returns in social good on the investment.

The needs of the State justify laws of compulsory education. A democracy can not be successful and progress if handicapped by citizens who are an economic charge, a social threat, and a political negation to all that promises good. Therefore it compels attendance at school until the severest of ignorance danger is past. But compulsory attendance would be of no more avail than seclusion unless the educational program contributes to the welfare of society. The very practice of compulsory attendance emphasizes the necessity of a program as highly contributory as possible to this end. Compulsion should continue at least until each student passes the neutral zone from liability to asset, and attendance should be permitted and encouraged until the law of diminishing returns is clearly operating. All through their courses students should be made conscious of the reasons why the State furnishes them free education so that they may gradually develop an understanding of their obligations. They should realize that secondary and further advanced education is not a natural right, which they may waste, but a privilege to be earned.

If the thesis of investment is accepted, it follows inevitably that measurement of the results of an educational program must be made in terms of its contribution to the good of the State. It is very much easier, of course, to develop a technique for careful measurement of acquiring and retaining facts that have been taught. Such a technique was long considered unnecessary or impossible, but it is now being tardily developed. A technique for measuring success in contributing to the welfare of the supporting State will prove more difficult, partly because results are usually delayed, partly because the problem is much more complex, but chiefly because, as before emphasized, we have never given enough thought to the matter to decide even with reasonable definiteness just what the desiderata are. When we have done that, which is inevitable and necessary for an intelligent and justifying program, we shall be in a position to develop means of measuring the results of education in terms of the purposes for which it is supported. It would not be a difficult task to find for this demand a technique quite as accurate as that which has for generations given general satisfaction in measuring achievements with academic facts. But a better one is needed, and it is reasonable to expect that the ingenuity of experts can in time produce it, provided they and the supporting public realize the necessity. It is a sad commentary on the seriousness with which we have considered education and the lavishness with which we have made an investment for it that we have been so little concerned with the kinds of dividends that it should pay and have demanded so little of definiteness in the way of accounting. Education, as truly as any other investment, should be required to justify itself by the return of definite dividends.

For such dividends the officials entrusted with the expenditure of public funds should be held strictly accountable. If they are not competent, they should be replaced. If others that are competent are not available, they should be developed. At the present the demand certainly exceeds the supply. Pending the development of a high type of expert such as the importance of the need justifies, much can be accomplished by directing the attention both of the professional body and of the laity to the seriousness of the undertaking and to the wisdom of advancing as rapidly as is possible toward a program that promises returns to the betterment of the State.

The officials in charge of the expenditure of public money for roads or other such improvements are held responsible and their success is measured in terms of the products that they tender. Their products are at the extreme of definiteness; they can be seen, measured, and tested by use. From this extreme we pass to the line of officials that are entrusted with peace and order, recreation, or health, objectives that are less definite but the results still measurable with relative ease. Such officials are continued in office and granted funds if they make a reasonable showing of results and manifest a program that logically promises success. At or near the other extreme of definiteness is the business of education. All that we can at present expect of the officials entrusted with this responsibility is that they show as clearly as possible their results, that they have a program that logically promises material contributions to a bettered social State, and that they manifest reasonable progress with this program. This we should demand. Without it the great investment of education will continue to pay inadequate dividends and ultimately will lose the support of its stockholders.

A program such as is indicated will doubtless require an outlay of investment far beyond what we have as yet known or conceived. That fact we may as well face frankly and at once. But despite the opposition now frequently voiced at expenditures for public schools, an increase, even a considerable increase, is neither unreasonable nor impossible. Our country is so rich that it has afforded in the past and will afford in the future anything that it needs and wants. The amounts expended for war and for hard roads would have been considered fantastic and impossible before the demands arose; but at need funds were found and appropriated, even with enthusiasm. Whenever public education is conceived as a public necessity, adequate appropriations for it will similarly be made. The returns from these investments will be tremendous, materially as well as spiritually.

Education is a necessity for the perpetuation of the democratic State and for the promotion of its interests. There is no other instrument for insuring these ends. Therefore it follows that whatever the cost the State must for its own salvation appropriate it. Industry has repeatedly shown the wisdom of scrapping plants, of reorganizing its personnel, or of undertaking new enterprises at staggering expenditures when such radical action was thought wise for increasing dividends. The corporations that were timorous of doing so have never achieved the prosperity of those that were intelligently daring. How much wiser is such a program for democracy!

The State has dimly had such a conception and has appropriated generously for the establishment and maintenance of schools. But it has confused any kind of education with that which promises to pay and does pay assured and large dividends to a bettered social order. The value of anything is determined by its contribution to use. Medicines that do not heal and foods that do not nourish are not cheap at any price. Laying out money for that which does not return good, and the maximum good, is an extravagance. Much of our expenditure for secondary education has been an extravagance because it was not directed toward a return of maximum good to either the individual students or to the investing State.

The chief item in the budget of increased costs will be for the employment of suitable teachers. During the past few years there has been much agitation concerning teachers' salaries and in justice they have been somewhat raised in amount. The best teachers are still inadequately remunerated; the poorest are tremendously overpaid. Uniform schedules will always result in this inequity. The plain fact is that there are not enough good teachers, even reasonably good teachers, to staff the secondary schools. There never will be so long as the public fails to comprehend the seriousness of education, until education by seriously undertaking the responsibility for which it is supported manifests its values in making youth better able and better disposed to contribute to the betterment of the State. No intelligent person knowingly permits an incompetent mechanic to tinker with his car, or calls in a less competent physician than he can afford to minister to his ailing body. And yet we have complacently or even with pride entrusted our children to teachers whom we have no evidence for believing more than nurses, policemen, and amateur practitioners in the art of instruction.

Professor Palmer once wrote in a precious document : "Harvard College pays me for doing what I would gladly pay it for allowing me to do." * It is such a spirit that is demanded of teachers. But more is demanded : they should be required to know and to live the good life, a rich life, and to work constantly and skilfully with the sole aim of developing each individual according to his natural aptitudes and capacities so that he can contribute maximally to the social good. Many teachers are working in this direction with conspicuous success. More will do so

* The Teacher — George Herbert Palmer and Alice Freeman Palmer. P. 5. Houghton Mifflin, 1908.

when the public as well as the profession recognizes that education is an essential for the
preservation and for the promotion of a happy
and prosperous social order. If such teachers cost
more, the money will be found. Teachers of any
other type are extravagant at any cost whatever.

If education were generally and truly considered a necessary investment by the State, teachers would more commonly be held in high esteem,
expectation of which has lured many into the
vocation. In the old Prussia, where, as has been
shown, teachers were known to have an important state function, they had high social rank,
higher by far than that reported in Middletown.
The more respected their social status, the better
the men and women are who are attracted. Understanding and approval of the thesis would
furthermore greatly increase the protection that
schools now have from interference of all kind
by selfish men or by misguided enthusiasts.

The implications stated sound, separately and
in the aggregate, as if a revolution would follow a general understanding and acceptance of
the principle, a revolution social as well as educational. And indeed there would if its application were immediately carried to a logical conclusion. A conviction that this is true has justified
this lengthy exposition. But material advance
seldom comes by revolution, least of all in edu-

cation. All that can be hoped for is that the discussion will turn attention to the necessity of justifying free education. Hitherto both the lay public and the professional expert have been too much content to take it for granted. The justification proposed seems most valid of all those that have been considered. It is easy to understand, at least in its general meaning, and so can easily be given popular explanation. Once accepted it will strengthen popular support and give direction to extended programs of improvement.

No honest thinker can reject it without substituting something better. Nothing so important as education is, to say nothing of what it can be made to be, is safe unless firmly founded, at least in the minds of the leaders, on some valid principle. It is easy to conceive of dissent from some of the conclusions drawn in following the proposed principle to what seem to be its logical conclusions; but such dissent, whether emanating from prejudice in favor of current practices or from other causes, should not blind one to the soundness of the basic reason for free public education, and it should stimulate him to think through for himself the applications to their logical results. When professional and lay leaders do this, we may confidently look forward to a steady elevation of educational practices and to a resultant improved social state.

V

During the past generation there has been in the United States such a development of education, especially on the secondary school level, as the world has never previously seen. We are amazed and proud as we contemplate the twenty-odd thousand high schools, many of them magnificently housed, equipment that compares favorably with that of colleges, the more than four million students that are enrolled and retained as never before, the laws that extend the privilege of free attendance even beyond school districts, the improved skills of teachers, the better personal relations with students, the concern for their welfare in a larger concept of education, the recognition of the importance of extra-curricula activities and their direction, and the increased importance of such subjects as general science, music, fine arts, and industrial education. We have seen, too, development toward a science of education, with objective measurements and a tremendous amount of fact finding, varied from the important to the trivial. As a result of researches and instruction there have been great improvements in governing legislation, organization, buildings, budgets, and administration. We now have better machinery for education than we have a conception of what education is. Along with this has come a constantly increasing public support, evidence of an enthusiasm that amounts to a fetish. The public believes in education almost regardless of what it is. It has appropriated generously for it without demanding an accounting in results.

All this growth is gratifying and conducive to a complacent pride. There is a disturbing element, however, one that gives concern regarding the values resulting from all the effort, the direction of progress, and the permanency of public support. When we ask, either of the professional schoolman or of the enthusiastic layman, for a justifying philosophy of education or even for a common-sense statement of what is being sought by means of the elaborate machinery, we find much indefiniteness and consequently an alarming disagreement on what should be the details of the program. What can be the worth of the physical plants, the large registrations, and the laudable efforts unless all the details are contributory to some broadly unified scheme? How can there result satisfactory dividends on the great investment if we have an educational conglomerate instead of an educational system steadily directed toward the achievement of a clearly seen social purpose?

Everything must find meaning in the end toward which activity is aimed, and that end is clear in too few minds.

The friends of public education, especially in secondary schools and colleges, may well be concerned for its stability in popular esteem. Always there are mutterings from those who are for one reason or another discontent and reluctant to continue or to increase appropriations. There is a constant possibility of an attack that might grow into a revolt. The neglect of a reasonable program for the sake of physical expansion has brought about conditions that would be difficult to defend. Ammunition is ready in the publications of scientific workers in the field, especially in the reports of objective measurements and of surveys. The possibility, however remote, of such an attack lays a strengthened obligation on the friends of public secondary education to renew their efforts to reform it from within lest it be weakened from without. However ineffectively and ambiguously it may have moved, it remains the only means that society controls for directing youth toward the ideals to which we are consecrated.

Assuming the validity of the thesis defended in this essay, a state's attorney might conceivably present against an educational authority an indictment for misfeasance in office and the misappropriation of public funds. This would consist of three main counts.

First, that the authorities have made no serious efforts to formulate for secondary schools a curriculum which promises maximum good to the supporting State. He could present all the literature in which curriculum reform is argued and find slight recognition of the obligation, certainly none such as its importance warrants. He could quote from all the new courses of study prepared by municipalities or by state governments and show that the principle is recognized in no such way as materially to influence the procedures of revision. And adducing the curricula and courses themselves, he could challenge their authors and defenders to show in what ways, directly or indirectly, immediately or ultimately, the subjects or the details of the subjects promise to influence youth to a maximum, or even to a better, contribution to the supporting State.

In defense might be set up the courses in health, public and private, which have recently begun to receive more than formal recognition, in civics, occasionally in economics, in general science, and the like; but to these would be opposed the usual and inordinate emphasis on foreign languages, mathematics, history that is unrelated in the minds of pupils or of teachers to any problems of current life, and details from practically all other courses, old or new. The dead wood of tradition and the lifeless units of false and formal "scholarship" are found in all subjects. The deplorable and blameworthy situation exists primarily because we lack an understanding of the purposes for which education is provided by the State. When there is agreement that it is a wise and a necessary investment rather than a kindly beneficence, it will have a sound foundation on which to rest and a plan by which to develop.

But the blame can not be laid altogether on the individual administrator or teacher. On the one hand he is beset by the influence of scholars, in their own ranks as well as in the colleges. Recognizing the values of what they have studied and enjoyed, the exercise of their fine intellects, they falsely assume that higher academic learning is inevitably profitable and that it is the only kind which it is worth administering to all youth. Even when they stop short of these extremes, they give such emphasis to traditional academic subjects as to make it difficult for others that may contribute in more effective ways to students of different aptitudes and inclinations. This statement is made with full appreciation of the values of scholarship, of the great contributions that it makes to civilization. Those competent to acquire, enjoy, and use it should be early discovered, usually in the junior high school, and forwarded skilfully in their progress. But the wastefully continued effort to make academic scholars of all, or even of a majority, of students is fair to neither class. It handicaps those that have the peculiar gifts, and it fails to produce in others the knowledge, skills, and attitudes necessary for their own optimum development toward greater effectiveness.

Partly because of the respectability of the traditional curriculum, especially on higher levels, there has developed a fetish of education. Recognizing that those who had in the past mastered the academic subjects have on the whole been successful and honored citizens — honored often because of a mystical veneration for powers not generally possessed — the public has falsely assumed that the very seeking, even without mastery and subsequent manifestation in use, is profitable to the individual. Feeling thus, the public supports education, and parents, who compose the part of the public most active in influencing support of the schools and who are ambitious that their own children shall have special advantages, usually with unconscious selfishness bring an irresistible pressure on school authorities to continue the old program. The results are so intangible and usually so remote that the failure of the investment, tending to the bankruptcy of the State, is not clearly seen. The mystical public reverence still gives to the traditional secondary education advantages for the individual that are not real for the State. The social prestige resulting from the passing of courses that contain no vital interest and later manifest no material influence on action or on character is mischievous and deceiving. It wastes annually millions of dollars of public money and precious time of students, and it deludes youth into a false sense of possession, which the world assuredly if gradually corrects.

A third reason why the individual administrator should not be too severely blamed is that before the tremendous and complex problem he is relatively powerless. Reform of the program requires primarily a sound concept of the purposes of education and of its responsibility to the supporting State. Even if he has that, he still needs a more comprehensive philosophy, which can be satisfactorily formulated only by the coördinated and long continued efforts of experts. This can be provided only when both the profession and the public realize the need and furnish the means. And even when a comprehensive philosophy is produced there must be long continued and expensive research to ascertain necessary facts which can be used in revising old procedures and in inventing new ones.

But even though the individual administrator or teacher has excuses, evidence is abundant that the program of secondary education, especially in the small schools but by no means in them alone, has never been intelligently formulated with any serious intent to profit the supporting State. This evidence can be found by any person who, laying aside his prejudices, examines either the curriculum as a whole or the details of the several courses of study. It is too evident to cite instances in this limited space or to give illustrations. Careful researches would only confirm what is obvious to common sense.

When confronted with the charge that he has made no serious effort to formulate a program contributing maximally to the good of the supporting State, the individual administrator could only plead *nolo contendere,* state his excuses, and throw himself on the mercy of the court.

The second count of the indictment would be that there has been no respectable achievement, even in the subjects offered in the secondary school curricula. Evidence on this count is abundant in scientific documents, especially in those that present the results of standardized objective tests. A seventy per cent achievement in mathematics is not respectable in schools; in business it would soon lead to bankruptcy or to the penitentiary. One half of our students after a year's study of algebra are reported * as unable to find the area of a circle when they are told the formula and the value of π and given all necessary data. In one state only half of the selected group who entered the university were able to find the value of b when given the equation $by = 2$. On three successive Regents' examinations the percentages of students who had begun the subjects in New York City high schools and who passed ranged from 30 to 79 in algebra; from 21 to 86 in plane geometry.

A smattering of modern foreign languages — and this is all that is gained by the vast majority of our students — is not respectable; it neither does nor can manifest itself in any material utility of reading or of communication. After one year's study of French in our high schools only half the students can translate so simple a sentence as *Je n'ai parlé a personne.*† 42.5 per cent of the students who elected French have dropped the study by the end of one year, and 79.5 per cent by the end of two. In reviewing the data collected from students of modern for-

* Hotz, H. G., First Year Algebra Scales. Bureau of Publications, Teachers College, Columbia University.

† Henmon, V. A. C., Achievement Test in the Modern Foreign Languages. Macmillan, 1929.

eign languages in New York City junior high schools, Wood says * that "we can not escape the suspicion that only a fraction of these 25,000 youngsters really belong in foreign language classes."

In Latin the results are as bad. More than three fourths of the students of the subject in the educationally progressive territory of the North Central Association of Colleges and Secondary Schools pursue it for two years or less, in which time they have merely made a start on the elements with which they might acquire substantial values. After one year only 50 per cent are reported † as able to translate a sentence of such elementary difficulty as *Illi homines duos amicos habebant,* and only 55 per cent can give correctly the complete conjugational classification of *videbat.* After two years half have advanced only to the ability to translate *Cum miles fortiter in bello pugnavisset ad domum profectus est* and 33 per cent to classify completely *posset.* It has been shown without any attempt by defenders of the subject at refutation, that the study of Latin in the majority of cases is more likely to interfere with good English ex-

* Wood, Ben D., New York Experiments with New-Type Modern Language Tests, page 8. Macmillan, 1929.

† The Measurement of Ability in Latin, Journal of Educational Psychology, 8:589 ff; The Lohr-Latshaw Test, The Classical Journal, 18:459.

pression than to contribute to it. Buswell and Judd show * that the best pupils from seven high schools learn to decipher rather than to read Latin. These selected pupils made as high an average as 50.8 eye fixations, with numerous regressions, in attempting to read each line of simple prose. With English prose they averaged from five to seven fixations.

When after a year of Ancient or of American history half the students are unable to tell who Solon was or to define the Monroe Doctrine, topics that are usually emphasized, we can have little faith that enough information is acquired and retained to make possible any substantial value of the kinds that are claimed. There is a paucity of objective evidence that history as it is taught makes any respectable return of dividends on the investment of students' time or of the State's money.

In English, to take only one other of the traditional subjects, abundant evidence exists that there has resulted in the majority of students no permanent taste for what is called standard literature. In fact there is more than a suspicion that a considerable number of specialists themselves actually prefer lighter and more ephemeral

* Buswell and Judd, Silent Reading: A Study of the Various Types. Educational Monographs, University of Chicago, 1922.

forms to those which they usually promote in the classroom. When three of ten seniors in superior high schools select * parodies on Tennyson's Bugle Song as superior to the original, and when a large number of seniors jointly rate The Story of the Other Wise Man and Helen Keller's autobiography far above The Ancient Mariner and Henry Esmond in permanent value and judge that from all the selections they have studied Dr. Jekyll and Mr. Hyde is least "artistic", one would be hard put to defend the investment as expended. Book reports † that when 900 freshmen at Indiana University were tested on an assigned passage of English prose, on which they had two days for study, only 27 per cent of the boys and 39 per cent of the girls could give the title of the chapter or formulate in any terms the chief problem discussed by the author. The average freshman boy was able to note and master only 34 per cent of the important points made in the assigned passage. The results in written English are in a large fraction of the cases shocking in their evidence of inadequate achievement.‡

* Abbott and Trabue, A Measure of Ability to Judge Poetry. Teachers College Record, March, 1921. Teachers College, Columbia University.

† School and Society, 26: 242–8.

‡ See, among numerous publications, Creek and McKee:

This is not the place to multiply the evidence, as it is easy to do, or to press the charge. Educators are generally aware of the failure and almost everywhere are working, often with exceptional ingenuity and skill, to improve results. But they are working against tremendous odds. With the increase during the past generation of inclusiveness until the secondary schools now enroll at least half of the adolescent population, there has resulted a heterogenity of abilities, both in kinds and in degrees. At first, standards were held high, with the result that the percentages failing were too large to be tolerated. Gradually two remedies have been attempted. One was an improvement of teaching methods, which on the whole has been more marvelously successful than most people, even in the profession, realize. A larger number of teachers are today demonstrating conspicuous skill in our schools than ever before. The second was a reform in the courses; much useless material has been eliminated, and what remains has generally been recast into a more teachable form. Requirements are in the traditional subjects much lower than formerly, however, and in the newer subjects they have been adjusted to the abilities of the students and have seldom reached a high level

The Preparation in English of Purdue Freshmen. Bulletin of Purdue University, December, 1926.

of demand, especially in organization for progressive difficulty and coherent unity. In those respects the older subjects still have a distinct advantage.

In spite of our declarations of the idea that secondary education should be furnished to all normal adolescents, and in spite of laudable progress that has been made in extending opportunity, it still remains highly selective. Several careful researches show that the children of the higher social and economic classes continue in high schools longer and in greater proportionate numbers than do those from less fortunate circumstances. And yet taxes are collected from all, the rich and the poor alike, that all may be advanced for the good of society. It is a paradox of democracy for the State to reach its hand into the pockets of the poor to procure funds for the advancement of those already blessed by nature or by parental heritage, and yet this is exactly what the State is doing. Children of the lowly are in large numbers discouraged from entering our high schools or are forced out of them chiefly because they do not have the peculiar aptitudes, interests, and capacities necessary for success in the limited curriculum so commonly offered and emphasized. But aptitudes, interests, and capacities they do have, and these are profitable to society in proportion as they are recognized, directed, and developed. Advanced education appropriate to each youth must be insured until he can profit no longer from the school, or the State is discriminating against some of its children and weakening its great investment.

While giving generous credit to the efforts that secondary school teachers have made to reduce failures, we must emphasize the fact that they have been successful in their campaign largely as a result of reducing their demands. The lowering of standards that a respectable percentage may pass is fair to students at neither extreme. Those with exceptional academic abilities are not challenged as they should be to the high accomplishments of what they are capable; those with abilities of other kinds are wasting their time in attempting a program for which nature did not equip them and in which they are doomed to insignificant achievements or to failure. The overlapping of standardized test scores indicates something of the unfairness of common practice; it is not unusual to find one fourth of a class making higher scores than half of the one a year more advanced. Influenced by the fetish of education, which they share with the public, teachers are still to too large an extent attempting the impossible task of putting a tremendous amount of heterogeneous ore through a process that was devised to refine only a limited kind. They have during the past few years been more successful in improving old subjects than in inventing new ones. Material advance will come only when they see and when the public sees that the schools are supported that the State may be perpetuated and improved. Then curricula pointing to this great end will be devised and success will be considered only such mastery as actually contributes to the bettered State. It is a saying as true as it is old that whatever is worth doing is worth doing well. The secondary school job is not now done sufficiently well to insure adequate dividends on the investment.

It is difficult when reading such evidences of lack of achievement to keep attention on the argument. Our secondary schools have failed, more lamentably than is commonly realized, in their attempt to administer the traditional curriculum, however greatly it may have been improved, to so large a proportion of the adolescent population as has been permitted and encouraged to attempt it. And in this failure they have squandered the public investment and weakened the State. In simple justice it should be emphasized that the schools have been remarkably successful in promoting the growth of gifted youth by the same curriculum. Probably never before have so many boys and girls actually learned foreign languages, mastered the elements of mathematics, developed abiding interests in the best literature, and acquired skill in both oral and written expression. Recognition of these facts should be made and generous praise should be given to the teachers who have masterfully contributed to such accomplishment. But while recognizing and rejoicing in it we must not forget that the great investment of education is concerned with all the raw material out of which the future State is to be made. In order that it may pay the reasonably expected dividends, it must develop each individual to similar accomplishment in fields in which he is most gifted by nature. This means far more diversification than is common and that is usually thought possible. But nothing less can be justified when education is seriously conceived as the chief means of preserving and promoting the State. "The acquisition, the understanding, the interpretation, the dissemination of the best — in any field — that has been thought and said in the world" is still a sound partial ideal in education; our thesis merely emphasizes for the greatest good the words *in any field,* which have usually had scant attention when the quotation is made.

The third count of the indictment would be that no effort has been made sufficient to establish in students appreciation of the values of the subjects in the curriculum such as to insure continued study either in higher schools or independently after compulsion ceases. There are several kinds of evidence to support this charge. It is found in the wasteful shifting from field to field in high school until enough "credits" are accumulated for graduation. This generally recognized tendency, which grows out of a failure on the part of students to recognize the values of what they have studied, is combated by requirement of sequences of subjects; but despite this, it has been shown that there is in a distressingly large number of cases a wasteful shifting from subject to subject with a consequent mastery in none, a lack of coherence in programs, and almost inevitable loss of most of the unrelated facts that were acquired.

Evidence is found, too, in the failure of students who enter college to continue there subjects that they have previously studied, often merely to satisfy requirements for admission. In one large college for women it is reported that only one girl in ten elects the subject which she has, by requirement, been studying for four years in order that she might prepare to gain from it the profit that mostly comes on advanced levels. The situation is similar in other colleges and regarding other subjects. It can hardly be maintained that values of elementary courses in foreign lan-

guages and mathematics are in themselves sufficient to justify the investment for them if they
are not continued by a considerable number of
students to achievements that permit profitable
use.* For exploration of students' abilities they
are too long extended and have too few immediate values. For revealing values they are un-
convincing, as is proved by the small number
who after compulsion ceases continue to seek
them. To a less extent the situation is the same
regarding other subjects of the conventional curriculum. It is not that they are not important
for students of peculiar gifts, for indeed they
are. It is, rather, that for reasons already stated
or implied they are overemphasized for too large
a fraction of the student body. The junior high
school has not been sufficiently developed to sort
the students early according to what lines they
may follow with most probable profit. And in
attempting more than can be accomplished, our
secondary schools have significantly failed to
create such attitudes of appreciation and consequent desire that subjects are continued adequately even by those most competent to profit
from them.

* Fifty-two per cent of the boys and girls who had
studied French two or three years in New York high
schools reported that they intend to continue the study
of the language, only about half of these because they
liked it. — Modern Language Journal, 12:15.

Evidence is found finally in the large number of men and women who on leaving school drop with relief and with finality all concern with subjects to which they have devoted months and even years of time. This results from failure to develop appetites and desires that insure a continuance of vocational or avocational activity. Too often, far too often, education comes to be considered something that is completed under compulsion and constant direction, instead of something that continues unendingly to make life more interesting and more intelligible. "The more good things we are interested in," said Francis Bacon, "the more ardently do we live." And it is only by independently continuing studies, to which formal education merely gives an introduction, that we retain and increase the power to respond effectively to the various important phenomena of culture.

There have been several reports of formal experiments that many have informally made concerning the retention by adults of what they had learned, or were supposed to have learned, in secondary schools. In one sense they are amusing; in another and a more important sense they are pitiful, evidences of failure of the great investment of education. For the most part, what is worth learning is worth retaining. Much that is or could easily be made important, either for utility or for increasing one's intelligent interests and for helping to forward them, suffers a slow but inevitable decay because no attitudes of appreciation and of desire for more of the same kind were ever set up. The excuse that other duties make further study impossible is usually a slim one, for we find time to do precisely those things that we like and that we consider important. No life can be rich that does not constantly increase in the number, variety, and depth of interests. No life is likely thus to increase unless in its youth education assumes the responsibility and reasonably is successful in creating attitudes that insure the continuance of study. Jean Paul Richter truly said, "If youth be not golden, age will be but dross."

No State's attorney is likely so to extend his duties as to present such an indictment of school boards and of school officials for misfeasance in office and for the misappropriation of public funds. We are probably safe from the penitentiary or from ouster proceedings on these counts. But this fact does not excuse us from the moral obligation to remedy the obvious and the disastrous defects in secondary education. Any one who is informed and not disqualified by self-interest for impartial judgment must recognize that the curriculum has not been formulated with the primary, or even with any serious,

intent of returning dividends to the investing
State through youth made better able and better
disposed to contribute to its betterment. He
must recognize the totally inadequate achievement by the majority of students of even what is
offered. Nothing less than mastery of the essentials can be satisfactory. And he must recognize the serious danger to public welfare in high
schools that create attitudes of complacency in
"having had" rather than in having, of "get-
ting by," and of relief when there are no more
compulsions to learn. This attitude is not naïve;
it is the result of what the schools teach and of
how they teach it.

Recognizing these facts, one very naturally
asks what should be done. A better question is
What should I do? The remedies that any single
individual, of the profession or of the laity, can
contribute seem so pitifully inadequate that in
despair he shrinks from taking on new responsibilities, for which he feels so little competence.
And yet it is only by individual assumption of
responsibility that the necessary coöperative effort can come. The beginning is unquestionably
in an understanding that education is a serious
business, a vital business for social welfare, and
that it is a great public investment, the most important that the State can make; therefore it
should be made to pay assured dividends. When

there is a general conviction on this fundamental matter, a conviction so real that it eventuates in action, everything else will follow in due course of time. Unless there is this conviction, progress will be slow, uncertain, and more or less fortuitous.

It may reasonably be asked why we as a people have never been more concerned with the reasons for public education. In the early Colonial days we were concerned. Devoted to their religion and hopeful of freedom, the Fathers established schools, feeling confident that if "that old deluder Satan" * were foiled by Scriptures correctly read, all good things would follow in order. In the various documents and laws repeated mention is made of "the promotion of true piety and virtue," of "service to church and state," though nowhere was the nature of the latter service defined, and Franklin advanced as one reason for his Academy the training of men to be magistrates. But not unlike earnest men of this day, our ancestors were so unreasonably convinced that "education," whatever its kind, would lead to all good ends that they left the details largely to the teachers, who being traditionally minded repeated to others what they

---

* A facsimile of the Old Deluder Law may be secured gratis by addressing the Graduate School of Education, Harvard University.

themselves had been taught. The faith of the public in education, then as now, was beautiful evidence of their hopes and aspirations.

In the beginning and for a long time afterward secondary schools were not free. The reasons why they finally became so are numerous and complex; they do not include a clear conception that secondary education was desirable and necessary for the perpetuation and promotion of the State — at least, in no direct and defined way. Once the policy of providing education beyond the elementary levels was accepted, for whatever reasons there may have been, it was maintained and developed through individual demand, local pride, and the same indefinite faith that motivated the Colonial Fathers. They saw that the educated man had advantages and frequently was a superior person and they concluded that his Latin and Greek were a cause; they were not keen enough to perceive that the very powers that made possible mastery of these difficult subjects also enabled him to overcome new difficulties and to solve new problems. Thus a fetish grew up, with the consequent multiplication of schools and improvement of facilities. The enthusiasm and the energy of patriotic laymen have been directed chiefly toward improving the mechanics that make education possible. When transgressing this necessity these laymen have naturally concerned themselves with details rather than with fundamental and directive principles.

The early objectives of good to Church and State, however clearly minted at first, have long since been rubbed down to mere discs of currency; and yet they still occasionally have value in influencing the program. They have produced legislation concerning the teaching of evolution as well as of the constitution. What we have lacked and what we seriously need is a conception of the fundamental principle, by both the profession and the laity, — not only a conception but also an approval of it so intelligent and wholehearted that it will furnish an enduring foundation and a directive force.

The one time when education was sincerely and thoroughly understood as being essential to the nation was during the World War. Because of this, curricula were modified, sometimes unwisely, by omission and by inclusion. Not only were the forces of the schools marshalled for the national good, but a Committee on Public Information included all of the population in its program. As soon as the armistice was signed, however, the Committee was abolished, adults were left to fortuitous and sometimes mischievous agencies of instruction, and the secondary school curricula returned more or less to the old norms. Too many schoolmen echoed the complacent ejaculation of one reactionary, "Thank God, now we can return to the job of real education!" But, as before said, if education is important for the preservation of the nation in war, it is even more important for its preservation and promotion in the enduring times of peace. The enemies, especially of decay, may be less obvious, but they are no less real and dangerous.

I believe in democracy, which means that the ultimate highest good for the people can come only through the active and intelligent participation of the people in formulating the rules for living. But a successful and progressive democracy is possible only if the people make provision for the education of youth not only in the accepted rules of conduct but also in such ways that they may contribute to their improvement. This means all youth, each one made maximally competent according to his natural gifts. The only instrument that society has for accomplishing its great end of preserving itself and of promoting its interests is education. Therefore I believe in education. However unplanned it may have been, whatever defects it may have, our schools have already contributed to society more than have all other agencies combined.

What they may contribute when so planned as to justify themselves in a modern world is greater, incalculably greater, good. In this faith, in this conviction, in this knowledge, we support the public school.

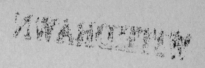